Brainpark

Brainpark

Anna Sanderson

Victoria University Press

VICTORIA UNIVERSITY PRESS
Victoria University of Wellington
PO Box 600 Wellington

First published 2006

National Library of New Zealand Cataloguing-in-Publication Data

Sanderson, Anna, 1970-
Brainpark / Anna Sanderson.
ISBN-13: 978-0-86473-543-0
ISBN-10: 0-86473-543-X
I. Title.
824.3—dc 22

Printed by Printlink, Wellington

To C.

Contents

Brainpark

In Rotterdam we lived on Zwaanshals Street. Zwaanshals meant swan's neck, the landlord had told us. I had trouble with Dutch vowels. I said the long 'a' like we would read it in English, as if a doctor had a popsicle stick on my tongue. People would repeat it back to me.

'Frans Hals?'

'No,' I would say, 'Zwaaanshals,' extending the 'a' further. This didn't help.

I did different kinds of work in Rotterdam.

I did teaching work. I went to Brainpark, a commercial suburb on the outskirts of the city to teach business English to corporate clients. Brainpark was a park of offices. Variations on the small contemporary office block were plotted around a ring road on undulating grass mounds. The office blocks were all about two to three storeys high; one might be glassy and curved, the next white and rectilinear. I assumed there were people working inside each one, as there were in ours, but I hardly ever saw anyone on the footpaths. Most people came and went in their cars.

As in much of Rotterdam, works of art were plopped down here and there. A red iron structure with ducks paddling around it rose slimily from the man-made pond in the centre of the ring road. What happens to ducks in the winter when the ponds freeze over? I wondered. My boss Herman told me they all clustered together and the movement of their legs in the water stopped the ice from freezing.

One day Herman came into the computer room with the panoramic view onto a neighbouring commercial park. This park, though, was still under construction. I was facing out towards it writing up student evaluations. He kissed me on the head and walked out again. I didn't react. I wondered what he saw as he bent over me, and tried to visualise my head from above.

Once a week I would go to the partially constructed park and teach classes to Shell employees. They were trialling a new kind of driverless shuttle which left from the train station and did a circuit round the various mirror blocks. It was like a truncated tramcar on wheels, and was able to sense where to go. It traversed the unsealed road slowly and hesitantly. As it was very sensitive to everything, you could be sure the shuttle would never run anything over. It would stop immediately if it detected something ahead. Once it stopped dead in its tracks for five minutes because a stray plastic bag had billowed into its path.

At Shell we did exercises from the textbook about virtual commuting. The picture in the virtual commuting chapter was of a remote stone cottage in the Scottish Hebrides. Apparently Shell was encouraging people to work from home these days. The students grumbled about this, although they didn't much like the crammed open-plan offices of the new building either. They talked about how in its early days Shell employees lived onsite in company housing. All your neighbours were Shell people too, and the company provided childcare and healthcare in the 'village', so you didn't need to go out much. No one seemed to be able to say if this would have been a good or a bad way to live.

Back at Brainpark, one client came weekly from a research institute across the road. He didn't really need much help; his English was excellent. He would always mention how wonderful his last English teacher had been, and I started to think he must have been in love with her, although he was probably just a generous person, because when we finished our lessons he gave me a lovely CD of Georgian Orthodox choral music. His company had co-produced the CD as a form of sponsorship. Georgia was one of the new independent states of the former USSR that his company had been assisting with becoming part of the European Union. They were helping the country with 'banking services, privatisation, development of small and medium sized enterprises, agricultural reform, new transport corridors and nuclear safety', the liner notes said.

I'd put it on at home. At certain points the almost shouting tones of the men's voices would create the effect of exalted distress. They'd reach a fever pitch, and their notes were clear and plain, almost harsh. 'What a racket,' my boyfriend would say, with his own type of tenderness.

I did my own work in Rotterdam, too. I had a desk in the bedroom of our flat. I meant it to be my workspace, and I would sit there with the window to my left, hearing Moroccan pop music coming from the video store across the street. I didn't get much work done though. In the winter it was better to be near the only heater in the house at the opposite end. Sometimes I would sit at the opposite end, but often there were people around. So I would go to the library.

The library was a building in the centre of town with all its plumbing on the outside like the Pompidou Centre. A rotund yellow pipe ran around the building. I would go there often and do my work, which involved finding material on Protestants, iconoclasm and The Reformation. I copied out quotes, mainly. 'A Puritan is thought to be a representative of a recurrent type of mind which is incapable of accepting anything from the life of the world as the bridge to the divine', it said somewhere. I wasn't sure what I was going to do with all this information.

I spent a lot of time 'not working' at the library too. One day I watched a documentary about sex work in Rotterdam. It was called *Hallo Schat* . . . I guessed that was what the prostitutes said to the clients when they approached the car, or when the car rolled by. *Schat* meant dear, or love. You could tell from the clothes and hair that the film had been made in the eighties. The prostitutes were working from a prefabricated building, set by the side of the motorway.

There were several women interviewed in this building.

Some of them wanted to talk about the really heavy things that had happened to them, and others kept it light.

One woman ate her ham and cheese sandwich and talked and laughed and drank her tea at the same time, gobbling it all up like a child and making it look delicious. Another one came out of the shower with dripping hair. She combed it, attacking it as she talked, and the knots wouldn't come out easily. Her speech took on the rhythms of the combing.

The last, who spoke at length, had been born a hermaphrodite. Her foster parents had decided she would be a boy. Somehow, after she got out from under them, she had had to become a woman, get back to being a woman, like it was a place. There she was. She said that a customer had said to her, 'I know you have AIDS—I want you to give it to me.' I watched her lips as she told this story. They seemed poisoned. She went to the paper towel dispenser before she went out on to the road, pulling out the paper and winding it around her other hand. She kept winding and winding until she had a wad the size of a balloon.

Lastly, I did sex work. I lay at nights in the apartment where I was by that stage on my own, listening to audiobooks from the library and waiting for the phone to ring.

'Ka-ate,' fat, wheezy Jan would say, 'I've got work for you,' always with exactly the same sing-song phrasing. A driver would be on his way pick me up. It never took me long to get ready. Since I wasn't very good with make-up, I just put on some lipstick. I always wore the same thing:

a black top with slits in the arms, a black skirt, and olive green rubber boots. One man said I didn't look like a prostitute, more like a girl going to a party.

I stopped after a few weeks. The last call-out was an American. He was very polite and somehow wholesome. He wanted me to run my fingers lightly over his back. He was rapturous about this as if it was better than sex, and as though he were letting me in on the arts of love.

'As light as you possibly can,' he said. He gave me a hundred-guilder tip.

Haesje van Cleyburgh

She is in the Rijksmuseum in Amsterdam. Rembrandt has painted her, simply dressed in a white cap and ruff. The plate-like white collar of starched and translucent linen is set into a double layer of perfectly even flutes. Its stiffness is only softened by the tiniest of undulations: a slight rise at the shoulder, and a dip under the chin.

She is positioned at forty-five degrees, within an oval frame. The oval of her shoulders under a black mass of garments repeats the frame's upper curve. It is as if a black oval casement window had been levered open. She is a number of geometric shapes stacked within an enclosed space: two eggs, a disc and a quarter sphere. What is the nature of the arrangement? Some rare quality may lie in the intersection of a diagonal plane and an ellipse. Something special may reside in the cross section of a cylinder.

Stand up close and all the colours appear. There is a sickly swirl of greenish yellow, a quietly roaring pink, a murky orange-brown. Stand back again and the colours become flesh. Except for that pivotal face (on which all else hinges and turns) the few other elements are black (the upper body and background) or white (the cap and ruff). The colour black and the colour white: the last outposts of colour. It sets the boundaries very wide.

The portrait is an image, but there is no image in her. She is absolutely free of glamour, like a washed potato is. It is a plump, rounded, evenly proportioned face. Her chin, a double or large single, is equal in dimension to her prominent forehead. Her eyes look rested, with slightly lowered lids. Wiry, greying eyebrows arch above them. The skin raised by these arches makes fine wrinkling at the temples, and around the eyes is dry and lined. You can understand the heaviness of her bones. Her cheeks glow, and are smooth, unweathered. A shallow dimple sits in her cheek out from a mouth with marginally upturned corners.

At times you think you see qualities: benevolence, impishness, primness, languidness, hollowness, something humbled, sharp, superior, simpering. As long as you keep looking, she keeps forming, and re-forming.

Flora

Even though the dungeon had been operating at the new address for a couple of years, Tara decided to have a grand opening party. The place was a work in progress anyway, as the new all-rubber wrestling room had only recently been completed. 'Rome wasn't built in a day,' the flyers for the party said.

Each of the mistresses had to choose a Roman goddess with a good story and have a costume worked out in time for the publicity photos to be taken. By the time I looked down the list pinned to the wall, written by Seven in her curvy childish writing, most of the good goddesses had been taken. Sonya was going to be the goddess of war and discord. Inga, whom Sonya had once described as a 'disturbed Gothic princess', knew she had to be the goddess of funerals. Tyra, who was described as both an 'African American' *and* an 'Amazon', was going to be goddess of the underworld. Lauren, an ex-Versace model who had sewn a brown leather body brace to wear with jeans and loafers, had chosen Minerva, the goddess of craft.

I looked down the list. Chance and abundance were also gone. Harvest, spring and marriage, not appealing. Fire seemed good, but came with home and hearth, doorways and sewers. Pastures seemed okay. Pales, the goddess who looks over the pastures.

I liked the idea that Pales just looked out and saw greenness. She seemed elusive and camouflaged, nymph-like, and I liked her stillness. Lauren said everyone had gravitated towards the goddess that was exactly appropriate for them. Pales was me because I was from New Zealand. But I wasn't quite happy with her. Firstly, she protected the lambs from the wolves. I didn't want to be protector of the lambs. And secondly, Pales didn't have a story. She watched and protected, but nothing *happened*.

Something had happened with Flora though. She'd impregnated Juno with the touch of her flower with no need for Jupiter or any male. Perfect. And I could still have the intricate leaf motifs painted on me that I had been planning for Pales. I imagined my costume would be body paint, dark green and leafy. I'd look like a tattooed lady, or a human fern.

As the goddess of fertility, my ovaries, which look like plants, would be drawn on the outside. I'd have a story, but I'd still get to be a plant. Plants don't perform; they absorb and grow.

Once I'd told my therapist about how I thought I could make this work my own, still be myself.

'It's bigger than you,' she'd said.

The photo shoot was a clash of visions. Emily, an ex-mistress, had been hired to style us, and Alexandra, an ex-mistress and super-passable transsexual, had been hired to do our make-up. Emily painted me with flowers. I became green and pink with plastic passiflora as fig leaf, a long wavy hairpiece and a colourful cloak of plastic blooms. Alexandra gave me light blue eyes, dark burgundy lips and severe blush streaks on my cheekbones so that my face looked thin. I thought I looked like a made-up corpse.

In my photo series I was to be paired with Juno, who is impregnated by the touch of Flora's special flower. Inga had been convinced to switch from being the goddess of funerals to being Juno. Juno was a more important goddess and an extremely jealous character. She scowled into the mirror as Alexandra arranged peacock feathers in her long blonde weave.

'I'm an artist,' Alexandra told Inga calmly. 'Have respect for my vision.'

I watched and shivered, wishing they'd hurry up, and unable to sit down because of my drying body paint and weakly attached flowers.

Inga had some kind of a meltdown at every photo-shoot and this one was no different. A healthy-looking recovered bulimic, she wasn't feeling too good about her appearance. Mostly, Inga had a proud line of patter about her body. She had unusually firm, gravity-defying, pointy breasts that everyone used to admire. Plus, she was the only blonde-haired, blue-eyed one amongst us, and thus very popular with the clients. Eventually Anna, our manager, took her away for a while and talked to her. I don't know what she said; maybe she reassured Inga she was beautiful, or the most beautiful. Eventually she came back prepared to start the shoot.

'I'm sorry,' Inga said to me later, in our of our few

moments of communication, 'I just have mad issues with my body.'

Tara was directing us. It was hard to pose my body and hard to arrange my face. For other photo shoots the formula had been back arched, knees slightly bent, head forward, chin in, toes out. It was like a perverse inside-out form of yoga, feeling wrong to look right. Now Tara instructed us to slouch forward and then roll back our shoulders and keep them where they ended up without moving the rest of our bodies. This was supposed to make our stance look natural.

Then she demonstrated how to arrange our hands. They were supposed to look relaxed and curved, and to hang down languidly at hip height and turn out. When Tara did it her hands looked as if they were a metaphorical door framing and opening her pelvic area in an inviting and womanly way. I tried but apparently it looked strained. She told me to shake out my hands as they looked tense. Being of average build, I had never felt scrawny before, but I did now. As I shook I thought of that Diane Arbus photograph of the skinny boy in Central Park whose tendons you can see in his wretched claws as he grimaces to the camera.

High Renaissance

There was a formula for analysing a work of art, for looking at it, and recognising the quality of light, form, content and style. I can't remember it now but I did then and it helped me in the exam: The High Renaissance 1500–1520.

Mrs Don was gaunt and delicate. She had a coarse-hewn quality around her brow and nose. She had spindly hands and wore circular peasant skirts pulled in at the waist. Her waist-length black hair was pulled back into clips at the sides, revealing intricate earrings.

She didn't wear make-up in a transformative way—smoothing out, widening eyes, bringing certain features forward and others back. She didn't change the shape of anything, but brightened what was there. She put pinky colours on her lips, which were thin and blue in the cold. She wore blue eye shadow. She coloured her features in, as if she were a line drawing.

Mrs Don tried to make art-historical concepts vivid, so that we would remember them. She would demonstrate contrapposto in front of the class. From the waist down, the weight is on one leg. From the waist up the weight is on the other side of the body. This was the key to the classical nude, a way to make the body look natural, and be in harmony.

Although just a device, contrapposto had a moral weight. Donatello's *David* with its campy, angular s-bend stance was a frivolous deviation from the limbs of Michelangelo's *David*, arranged as they were in classical harmonies.

The Maya Grill

It was still raining outside but very warm. In the restaurant it was cold with air conditioning, and I was seated right next to a whirlpool. There was a blue light at the bottom of this round hot-tub-sized pool, which was ringed with blond stone slabs. It was making glistening sounds and no splashes. Three little boys in T-shirts were standing at the edge of the whirlpool looking in.

'It's supposed to go all the way down into one . . .'

'I mean, yeah, what will real fire . . . it's a whirlpool—'

'Stick your finger in it's warm I told you that!'

'Squash! Squash! . . . Squash!'

'Let's try to make the whirlpool go the other way . . .'

'Ow! I almost got one! I got like, this section going.'

For a second I smelt a man's cologne. It might have been the waiter as he moved past me, or perhaps it was the man seated to my right, solitary, and the waiter's movement had pushed the perfumed air across the divide.

The meal came superhumanly fast. Almost everything on my plate was yellow: the fries, the fish, the zucchini, the cornbread, the butter, the olive oil and the candle shedding the light that glinted in my fork and along the fanning ridges of my fancy knife handle, and the flat blade of the butter knife.

The man across the divide checked his glowing blue phone while he drank his chilled rosé, dangling the glass by the rim with his fingers. There was another waft of cologne.

That afternoon during the thunderstorm I'd decided to go and swim in the pool. I was excited because I thought it would be deserted and wet and beautiful. In this Floridian Disneyworld where everything was artificial, lushness still crept around. Real plants were growing out of the soil and real rain splatted on their leaves.

We would always go to the beach during thunderstorms in New Zealand. The sea would be soupy and chaotic, full of seaweed and disturbed sand. I trod along the smooth red paving to the pool in just my togs, as what was the point of bringing a towel into the rain.

Then I remembered how in a thunderstorm in Ohio everyone had cleared the pool and gone inside. I went and asked the young woman at the gym desk if she thought it was safe to swim.

'Lightning strikes every thirty minutes,' she told me, as if I could wait for the last bolt and then get in.

A little girl came over with her mother to look in the whirlpool.

'Da! He he he he he he he he. Da! He he he he he he he he. Doo! Doo! Doo!'

'This is . . .'

'Mommy, you see white stuff in here? What is that under there?'

'It's the light! Can't you see, the light?'

'Isn't there something else under there?'

'I told you . . .'

There was another waft as the man took another sip of his rosé.

'That's real!'

'It's freezing. You know if you jumped in there, you'd be very cold.'

'Let me see, let me see, let me see, let me see!'

The blue light glowed a cold, police blue at the bottom, but the rest of the water seemed black. The water was calmer in the middle. Fat, oily ripples moved there, whereas around the outside it creased and cross-hatched. The man got up and left, walking with his hands on his front pockets. I smelt nothing. The chair back was cold when I leant against it. The whole place was cold. I reached over and put my fingers in the magnetic currents of the whirlpool. It was slightly warm.

Difficulty

I knew she was Jewish, but I asked her as I was going out what her religion was.

'I'm . . .' She searched for the term, and with hint of self-parody, '. . . *interfaith*.' Then she closed the door on me for another week. Shelley was a psychotherapist on West 14th Street I'd been going to see for the past few months. I had gone to her church in an office block in midtown. The church was New Age and quite interactive. You did little ice-breaking exercises with the people sitting around you.

'I didn't really like the hugging part,' I told her later.

'You get used to it,' she empathised, warmly.

Shelley was training me to know what I was feeling. She wrote down a list of the words I was allowed to choose from to describe my emotions during sessions:

MAD

SAD

GLAD

SCARED

If my eyes started to tear or my voice quavered, she would ask me what was coming up for me.

'It's kind of complicated . . .' I would try to say.

She would point to the list. 'Mad, sad, glad or scared?'

'Mad?' I'd say, hesitantly. 'No—sad. I think.'

Christ as a Man of Sorrows

(Painted in the style of Jan Mostaert, 1520s.)
He is looking through his tears. His eyes are swollen, brimming, overflowing. The whites and rims are red from crying. The fat film of tears coats his eyeballs and enlarges them. His mouth is open and you can see the edges of a lower line of teeth, and behind them a shadowed tongue. His lower lip has dry ridges and the beginnings of a deep crack at its centre.

Perfectly formed tears, more viscous and pronounced than normal ones, slide down his cheeks. They sit roundly on the surface and hold an image of the piece of skin underneath, lit and magnified. There are others too, pale red and smaller, more watery, tinted with blood.

This is a battered body, and yet there is no real friction, no evidence of resistance. Nothing in the image weighs heavily or catches or splinters or snags. The instruments of torture and the blood and tears they cause, grow out of him as painlessly as a nail grows out of a fingertip. The crown of thorns, shaped into its infinity symbol, leaves an even red blood rub underneath as if it was simply casting a shadow on to his brow. The thorns, rather than piercing, seem to float in the skin of his forehead as if it were creamy water. The golden rope knotting his two hands together in a cross over his chest seems like a big soft caterpillar nestled snugly around his wrists. His drapery folds thickly around his shoulders, remaining weightless, possessing a hint of marbly luxuriance.

Here there is something like syrup in my joints, something like the first molecular movements before waves of nausea. It is because of looking into a crying face and wanting to cry too. There is something suspicious about wanting to share this, wanting to acquire a little of this tragedy for myself, to wear.

Psalm 31: *Thou hast known my soul in adversities.*

I cannot take the melodramas of my own life too seriously because they are almost fictional hardships; they are like images. I must get away from my own body, which is also like an image. Because I cannot see my own soul, I cannot track and register its movements. What kills it? What feeds it? I am in such remote communication with it—who knows?—death blows could go unobserved.

Saint Jerome said it: *God looks upon the heart, we see only the face.* I look at this image of him, who both moves and rivets me and thus seems to pull me apart. All the same, I do not trust these effects. His face is a schematisation of suffering. It leads to an almost cartoon-like idea of suffering. It leads you to think people are OK when they don't cry. It takes away your powers of subtle perception and, in doing this, takes away capacities for depth and agility in compassion, which should be ever increasing to infinitude.

This is why the Man of Sorrows is so essential, and of no help. He is essential because he expresses everything that is important for a human being. And he is of no help because he is expressive. I need people's opacity and inexpressiveness to be better able to feel a sea of possibilities in them, because the idea of what is in them hasn't been channelled off and distilled as it has with him. He is of no help because in this way he seems like a window but becomes a wall, and then he is simply another thing that needs to be seen through.

This idea that all must be seen through can only be a curse. It rapidly engulfs everything and leads to me, staring at my own skin in an equal unrecognition, as if it might as well be skin constructed with oils on oak from the sixteenth century.

Interior

Drunk and jealous, I threw a glass in the direction of my ex-boyfriend.

'Get the fuck out,' he said. I went.

Once home, I got out the kitchen knife. The slit gaped to reveal a bumpy pink surface of muscle, with white streaks of fat cobwebbing over it. I went to the 24-hour Duane Reed and bought bandages, tape, Neosporin and that orange antiseptic that other children used to get on their knees at school.

I washed the blood away. Surprisingly, it stayed away. As I tried to close the cut, the skin lifted off the muscle and I could see dark space between them. Shadow. I made butterflies out of tape and, holding shut the edges, laid them across. Because of the greasiness of the Neosporin, the tape wouldn't hold and the cut sprang open again. I cleaned the grease off the edges, not wanting to look at the muscle, feeling I was seeing a wrong view.

Eventually I got it taped up, then bandaged.

Tintagel

The passageways of Columbus airport stretched out like long corporate corridors, serious colours and glass. There were comfortable blue weave seats, and windows with expansive views onto car parks and escalators. I waited facing empty baggage carousels, a thirty-two-year-old woman from New Zealand, and occupied myself with how to sit on the seat. I sat up straight and prim; slumped, teenaged and casual; then sat up straight again. Not many people came past.

I found them going down the escalators. On the phone, Deb had a resonant, thickly encased voice and a motherly attitude. Here she was now, maybe ten years older than me. She was saying something to a boy who had to be her son as they came down the escalator. He was flying something. There were no formalities to our meeting. She didn't engage in polite conversation so neither did I.

'Don't overwhelm her,' she said to Josh as he showed me Robowolf, a wolf that turns into a motorcycle. There was a physical softness to her. A softness of white bread and gentle light. We got lost inside the airport, walking up and down the stairs trying to find the right car park level. We found it eventually by a kind of controlled accident, much as we had found each other by the escalators.

Conversation in the car was mainly Deb talking to Josh and quips about lack of coffee. Josh was given the task of holding a large plastic coffee gulper, the coffee she was allowed to drink after her urine sample had been given. The seemingly endless explanations of parenthood: 'When I was young we used to make spaghetti sauce from scratch.'

'If you've had enough of him, tell him. He can deal with that. He knows to respect people's space.' She told me this as she went in to give her sample at the homoeopathist, leaving us in the waiting room. I said yes but I couldn't do it, so arranged blocks. He wanted the blocks arranged in conjoined masses of yellow, blue, red and green.

In the car again, Josh leant his warm silky head on my arm, and let Robowolf go up and down my leg, or swim through the air in front of us.

'Is that metal or clear?' There was a hexagonal insignia with cloudy reflections sticking up from the bonnet of the car. I couldn't tell if it was reflecting the silver of the car, or if it was actually silver.

'Wow,' said Deb. 'I don't know. I've never noticed that before.'

Many dogs came out to greet us when we swung up at Tintagel. Megan picked her way with bare feet over the gravel.

'Mom, I cleaned out the fridge, can I go to Melissa's for a swim?' She said hello to me making brief eye contact, but lightly, easily.

'If you give your mother a hug.'

She pretended to suffer a hug in the bear arms of her mother.

'Isn't she beautiful?' Deb presented her, looking with me. 'Do you know what Christiam said? He said you were opulent.'

I wouldn't have thought of that word but she was opulent, with her long curls, puppy fat in tight lo-rise jeans, and glitter lip gloss.

The property ran like a tongue or a tie unfurling between the road and the river. The Scioto. The house in front of us was a nondescript form in dull stained wood. Decorations led to the door: carved rocks, whirligigs, metallic bulbs. The doorway was crammed with panting bodies wanting to get in but not allowed. I waded through them, my hands grazing hairy backs.

In the door a plaque with the name Tintagel on it sat on a piano. There was the gurgling of fish-tank oxygen, and a cat stepping gingerly around pot plants in the window box.

'Her name is Anklebiter,' I was told. She sat, ladylike, little paws resting close together, a mottled strawberry roan.

I was given a quick tour. Through the hallway we passed a ball of fluff in a smelly glass tank filled with sawdust, not moving. In the bathroom there was a laminated landscape and a teenage poem about the depths of hell. Through the hallway into the big open kitchen, a twisting sweet potato projected taut reaching sprouts, and big dog bowls clustered underneath a birdcage containing a parrot. The dogs' names were Karina, Rascal, Prometheus and

Garth—huskies and collies. I got used to seeing Karina always outside against the shady wall of the outbuilding, looking uncomfortable, with her tender, bony, sighing ways. They thought she might be part wolf.

A television area with a soft couch and chairs arranged around a plastic children's table led through to the outside and where I was to sleep. We sat in the kitchen for a little while before I went down there.

'One thing I'm going to pretty much insist that you do is the centrepiecing. Once you know how to centrepiece, it'll really help you a lot.' I imagined cutting pieces of white paper to make lacy decorations.

My room was the middle of three outbuildings which sat down toward the river. The room was Tantra's. She had once given me her business card, which described her as a mystic and seer. During our first phone reading she told me she'd been born with an open mind. I had called her up in Ohio from New York and she spoke for an hour as I sat on my boyfriend Kevin's crisp white duvet and listened. She didn't need me to say anything. She was reading my cellular field.

Afterwards, she can never remember what she's said, but she sent me a tape of the hour and told me to listen many times, to steep myself in it like a tea bag in boiling water.

Now as I slept in her room, she was in Hawaii, walking up the sides of volcanoes, feeling orgasmic, she'd said to me on the phone. Her room was an aubergine colour, lined with different rugs, a Navajo type thing and one I imagined was horsehide. I made an inventory of everything in the room, as a portrait of her. There were 101 things in there.

In the evening I lay on the bed and read *The Adaptable Man*. I thought it was a bitter story. The room was cave-like, with the only window right by the door and with the bed at the far end. I closed the window and the room heated up but at least the mosquitos couldn't get in.

I got up in the middle of the night to pee. Not wanting to disturb the household, I found a piece of grass near the wooden steps which connected the outbuildings. Every night I did this Garth, the most scatterbrained collie, woke up and came with me, excited for the company. Every time I peed in the same spot, and every time there was a pungent plant very nearby, smelling like basil. In the day, I would see a scorch mark on the earth where the grass was dead.

During the day everyone went about their own business. I cooked or did some gardening. I watched TV with the kids sometimes; *SpongeBob*, programmes about owners trying to train their dogs, and a cartoon about a boy who had actual tiny fairy godparents with wings.

I wondered what the kids thought of me, but I knew they were used to guests, and they didn't seem too curious about why I was in their house. I was reminded of what I'd thought about that young woman at the Himalayan Institute. The drink-of-water girl, I'd called her to myself.

Although I'd known her name was Julie, she had put no name in the brass label-holder on her door, but had stuck a carved wooden 'ohm' symbol next to it. She was able to manage only small steps in her soft slippers and yellow tracksuit as she moved through the corridors. I wondered what she had, and thought it might have been anorexia or chronic fatigue, or one of those mystery illnesses. I never saw her interact with anyone. She was exempt from the normal social rules.

Her presence was so slight, it was almost like she'd literally faded. I wouldn't have been all that surprised if I'd looked at her and discovered I could faintly make out things through her body.

The people at Tintagel shared a theory about people who didn't live within the boundaries of their skin. Deb called them Sentient Beings. She wanted to write a book and call it *Care and Feeding of Sentient Beings*. She felt that Sentient Beings were part of a global spiritual vanguard, which was only going to grow and grow, until it was normal to be one. It was an evolutionary shift, as she saw it. At Tintagel we took our lessons where we found them: internet spiritual communities, the Bible, The Landmark Forum, *The Lord of the Rings*, *The Matrix*. We watched movies in which there were Sentient Beings, usually women finding life on earth torturous, like Jodie Foster in *Nell*, or Nicole Kidman as Virginia Woolf in *The Hours*.

Deb and her husband Russ got into an argument about *The Hours*. Russ couldn't believe that the Julianne Moore character who had so much trouble with baking her husband's birthday cake, walked out of her life and never saw her family again. It really irritated him that she did that. He thought she could have 'become herself' without such drastic action, ignoring the fact that there would have been no story in that. Deb said a person might well do that now, but that woman was living in the fifties.

Russ had a moustache just like Ned Flanders, and a wobbling arc of skin underneath his jaw; a perfect upside-down mound. He spoke with a kind of deliberate equanimity that sometimes came off as monotonous. He was more of a conventional Christian than Deb, who was more oriented towards 'spirit' in whatever form it took. Once, when Russ and I were in a Walmart café having a snack, I asked him if he had access to the language of tongues when he wasn't actually speaking in them.

'Oh yeah,' he said. 'Djhfgdslf yriluglaylbiu jdrhfjkerb.'

'Could you explain what faith is?' I asked him. He pointed to the waxy coke cup on the table.

'Try to pick it up,' he told me. I picked it up.

'See?' he said. I did see, but I still didn't get it.

Russ taught me how to do centrepiecing. 'It actually *rewires* your brain,' he said of the exercise, with a kind of incredulity people use to describe a new product. It was a flow chart type of exercise involving post-it notes and drawing arrows between one thought in a bubble which *allows for* the next, *invites* another, and *establishes* yet another. I started doing these all the time. 'Uninspired and uninspiring,' one might start, '*allows* for dark times, *invites* have their own quality *establishes*, variety.' Or, 'This morning touched surfaces, *allows for* they are always there, *invites* meditate every morning *establishes* beginning of a discipline.' The rigid structure for thought was restful.

One night Beryl, a singer and artist who drew people's energy signatures, came to visit with her daughter.

'Honey, you're in my energy space,' she'd say when her daughter pestered her. The first time she'd say it like a fact. The second time would be more like a warning.

She said to the others about me, 'It feels so great to know I would have no compunction about reaching down and pulling her up.' I didn't know where she would have been and where I would have been and what she would have been pulling me up out of, and I felt too tired to begin to ask her.

A lot of the time at Tintagel I sat down by the river or on the mysteriously named Celebration Porch, boat-like, looking at the river over the sea of grass. When I sat down there, the river was close and I could watch it ooze past carrying tufts of cotton and the occasional unidentified submerged thing.

I worked on my cross stitch, a 'NZ Bellbird' for a friend's new baby, wrote letters to people, or notes for myself. From behind the porch railings, leaning and peeling my sweaty forearms off the formica table, I could see the fish landing on the surface of the river and sinking down. I never saw them jumping because my head was looking at pen and paper and only lifted upon the splash. Actually, since I only saw the splash it could have been anything—a leaping beaver or a dive-bombing kingfisher. It sounded like a slapping fishy mass though—I imagined holding it in my hand as it curled left and right like a muscle removed from the body.

Josh came down, bored in the school holidays, wanting

me to go for a swim in the pool again. I was looking at a fallen hanging ornament. It was a tangle of coloured threads lumped over the splintering porch railing. It must have come down in the rain. I planned to untangle it, thinking in a shrouded way of horses' manes.

'Do you like this rainbow thing?' I asked Josh of the lush, silken heap. He came over, half touched it and said 'Its' or 'It's been . . .', then spoke of something else, in the way children have of dismissing what is not alive to them.

I brought down a piece of Josh's Yogi Bear birthday cake and ate it on the porch. The square I got had creamy white frosting, easily messed up, covered with a mist of tones graduating from green to blue. A thick chocolate stripe of piping formed a tree trunk. The light-as-air cream showed the frozen motion of the hand of the froster. I moved it around to see the white piped waves along the outside edge and got the sweet smell of sugar. The cake was beginning to perspire. I broke the sponge and it crumbled apart in light hunks.

A walk

It was getting late in the afternoon. I went for a walk down Anderson Road. I was scared going along the road, keeping a distance from dogs and cars. The grass of the shoulder was bouncy and scratchy under my roman sandals. A car drove past. Shiny and slowly. What were they doing here? They turned into a house further up the road.

The Ohio sky was big and pastel and the landscape unthreatening. Little detailed woods, small leaves, everything with a fine grain. I walked past two cows in a small corral. Small cows, looking curiously. The house beside them was beige and huge. Looking at this landscape was simple. You could either look across at the land or up at the sky. Everything seemed known and accounted for.

It felt good to have no things to carry. No bag no sweater no money no sunglasses no keys. My feet crunched on the gravel. A deer jumped easily and high in front of me, and darted away as if it was only using a tiny proportion of its immense nervous energy.

My mind was daunted with frightened thoughts and instructions to self: 'walk with those sprigs through the soles of your feet', 'breathe', 'I hope the person in the car doesn't look at me', 'they are going into their house and life'.

I walked around the bend and saw a trailer home. It was one of the models I wouldn't have thought were trailer homes because they have pitch roofs and skirting and shutters and seem solid. Out the back was a pool raised from the ground like a large tin can. A slide went into it. Teenagers were sliding in, laughing, holding themselves differently when wet, pulling a swimsuit off a body to make a bubble of air.

I saw a long corrugated building at an upcoming bend in the road. There seemed to be some kind of production going on there, from the constant whirring it was emitting. The whirring got louder as I neared. The building was completely unmarked, so it didn't seem like a factory exactly. There were conveyer belt chutes connecting the building with big vat structures on legs, either moving stuff in or out, and also two ramps. Nervous that someone would drive past and ask me what I was doing, I walked over the grassy expanse to where there was a little window cut in the vast corrugated wall.

As I came to peek in the window I heard a few snorts and thought pigs, before my head appeared at the window and wild shrieks let out. I ducked back. There were not just a few pigs but a sea of them, packed in wooden pens right down to the far end. The alarm of the few by the window triggered a chain of upset and the building reverberated with it. My head caused this, I thought. Why are they so upset? Don't they see humans? No, they probably didn't. They must have been fed automatically, by those whirring conveying machines. They probably came up the ramp at the beginning of life and down the ramp at the end. I went back up to the window, and stayed there this time. Gradually they had all calmed down, and didn't seem to mind my head any longer. I was struck by how clean and fine looking they all were. And pearly pink.

Arcosanti

You should always take every opportunity you get, my sixth-form English teacher told me. Her name was Ms Larkin and she had a pointy nose and round, flushed cheeks with freckles. Her black hair was a permed frizz. She often wore an emerald green synthetic tube skirt and black high-heeled shoes. She had taught in schools in the poorer suburbs of Auckland, and told us we North Shore kids were spoilt and sheltered.

When my friend Isobel suggested I fly to meet her in LA and drive in her cappuccino-coloured VW van to Arizona to visit Arcosanti, I went to the library. I didn't know anything about this architectural experiment in the desert near Phoenix, except that Tantra's daughter had worked there for a while as a volunteer.

I looked up Arcosanti in in the catalogue. The architect was Paolo Soleri. I liked his titles—*Space, Time and Simultaneity in Utopia: An Eschatological Probe*, and *The Bridge Between Matter and Spirit is Matter Becoming Spirit*— but they weren't in circulation so I got out the one big Soleri book there was, to bring on the road. 'This book is about miniaturisation,' said the forward to *Arcology*, the awkwardly shaped, lime green book that was too long to fit in my bag. Inside it cities were drawn like giant alien jewels articulated infinitely, plunged into the earth like a tombstone, a tooth in a gum, or an iceberg in water.

Three weeks later we drove through the gates of Arcosanti. It sat on the edge of a giant fissure in the mesa, looking out onto pale green grass, small trees and crumbly rocks.

We went on a tour of the community with a young architecture student who was living there with her boyfriend. There was still plenty of scaffolding and areas of raw earth. Construction had begun in the seventies and was still going. The aesthetic was of the seventies: modular, with lots of round doorways and windows. Progress had been slow because everything was handmade, and because of a reliance on volunteer labour, mainly young people wanting experience in their fields. Interest had flagged in the eighties, apparently. A cynical decade. But starting in the late nineties, activity had started to get up to its original levels.

The place seemed industrious that day. Electronic musicians were rehearsing in the sound shell for the upcoming Space Music Festival. Some students were making moulds for bells from local clay. Others were using clay moulds to cast bronze bells. The gift shop was crammed with these bells, and with publications and artwork by Paolo Soleri. I bought postcards of his design for an *Asteroid encased by a city in space*.

After lunch, served by still more students, I walked down a little track to a space underneath the main building, which looked out towards the mesa. Sitting under the shade of a concrete cube, the wind blowing lightly around its legs, I put my feet up on a rock. Sharpish stones jutted into my buttocks, making me visualise their doughiness. My dreams from the night before came back. Next to me was a circular concrete pool. It was full of dark water with goldfish. Green reeds were growing up out of the water like insects' legs, and growing downwards too, into the dark world which was both reflection and volume.

There was a piece of piping in the underside of the building, directly above the black goldfish pond. A drop of water from it plopped moistly into the pond. No water was wasted here in the desert. I looked up again and saw a hornet's nest attached to the open pipe. The nest was grey and cellular, much like the Arcosanti buildings. The little insects were crawling around on it, the colour of tigers. It wasn't enough to move for, but at the same time I didn't feel so relaxed anymore. Every time I heard movement I looked up.

Remember what the gestalt therapist said, I told myself. I had sat in her big stuffed chair with the blankets I'd tried to smooth out before I settled in for my session. The previous person had roughed them up, and it had seemed like I would be sitting down in the embers of some stranger's turbulence. She had asked me to close my eyes and concentrate on breathing. After a while, she'd said to become aware of the chair I sat in, and let it take some of my weight.

The ground was hard with the gravel spiking into my bottom, but I tried to let it support me. I tried to decide to let the earth hold me. My view went out to the dip and rise of the mesa, and the idea of the plateau beyond, and

I saw a hornet out of the corner of my eye. The hornets had long tails which looked like they held a vicious sting. This one let itself drop like a stone from the nest into the goldfish pond. I thought it might have been hunting, like a bird for fish, and would drag some smaller insect out, but it didn't appear to have anything as it surfaced and skated on the water, its legs making little dents like it was on oil or sponge. It climbed onto the rim of the O with a globe of water in its mouth, a miniature crystal ball, then flew away.

Phone reading

You're pulling into yourself but its not like you're withdrawing. It's like a violin pulling its strings into itself so they have pristine sound, you know? You're honing into being in touch. It's going to have an effect of opening the doorway into the deepest part of your design; it's almost like bringing you through yourself, as if you yourself are a portal.

I'm staying outside of imagery, because the worst thing I could do is create any kind of imagery right now. I want to strengthen that part of you that doesn't need to see. You carry an embodiment of some kind of ancient understanding, where you didn't have to use regular eyes. What I keep noticing is how often the word 'blind' or 'don't look' shows up. I really think it's because your sensory systems for a huge amount of your being here on this earthly plane didn't require sight. I doubt if it required any of it: taste, sight or hearing or any of the five senses.

Where you come from, they knew how to transubstantiate, which means they were capable of not losing consciousness even thought they lost their physicality. You and others put yourselves in a state of suspended animation.

The torque is what fascinates me. Literally, you're using the persona you're inside of, you're using that to try to get in the torque and un-torque it, and it's a fairly impossible job. But not to seek to do it is hopeless.

If you can imagine the Lady of the Lake and she's underwater. She has long hair, she's in the water, she's coming up, moving in slow motion and her long hair is flying through the air and the water's coming off it as her head's coming up. If you can feel that energy before she just totally comes out of the water, that's the feel state of your soul. When I talk I have to give you imagery but it's the feeling of that imagery that gives you who you are, not the lady coming out of the water with the hair. And that language of feel state is so ancient and so old, and now we live in the language of description which I find exceptionally brutal.

Over the last three or four years, you're starting to . . . sorry, it's a very Tennessee way of saying it, but you're starting to get with the programme. It's kind of like 'Oh well, I'd better consider there's something going on here, because if I keep operating at the affect of it I'm going to be in a lot of trouble'. You haven't quite sorted what's going on, but from a mind point of view, from a thinking point of view, Honey, I don't think you ever will. I don't think it's thinkable. What it is, is feelable.

The desert

Chris Kraus mentioned female abdications from art careers in her book *Video Green*.

> *I'd often wondered why so many of the confrontational, conceptual female artists who were Burden's prominent contemporaries in 1971 have disappeared in middle age to live around New Mexico in teepees, or become massage therapists or cranial sacral healers. What makes rage become New Age? By all logic, these women now should be our leaders.*

Why did Kraus think those now anonymous women weren't our leaders? *We* must be people in the art world, for whom losing prominence in art is a form of disappearance.

A person is like a radio frequency that gets picked up here and there, then lost elsewhere. Anonymity only works from a fixed position.

Ingmar Bergman wrote about anonymity, lauding the way people of all classes and occupations, like trails of ants, selflessly rebuilt Chartres Cathedral in the Middle Ages. 'It is my opinion,' he wrote, 'that art lost its basic creative drive the moment it was separated from worship. It severed an umbilical cord, and now lives its own sterile life, generating and degenerating itself.'

Miro

While looking methodically through hundreds of art postcards, I kept finding scenes built up through shoals of bright fine marks moving as patterns. Everything was articulated equally; the air was patterned, as were rows of corn. Different substances had equal degrees of solidity. That way clouds were architectural, and a house wobbled liquidly down one side.

They were Miro paintings. It was earlier work, still figurative.

I had boxes of postcards at home. They weren't for sending, and I never pinned them up. The stockpile would grow and grow.

I bought *Nude with Mirror* (1919). In the image an unclothed woman sat in a room with a curtain. She sat on an embroidered stool, holding a hand mirror out in front of her face but not looking into it.

There was nothing psychological going on. Her hair formed smooth lumps at the top, and had the felty look of a bowler hat. The plait was solid and plump, like a loaf of bread.

I equated the rust-coloured background with a wall, but really it was just a block of colour. It overspilled itself, brimming into the picture without breaking its bounds, meniscus-like.

The stylised festoon of curtain hung down and intersected with the woman's shoulder like two sets in a Venn diagram. The rust-coloured fabric, where it intersected with the flesh-coloured arm, stayed rust-coloured, but started to behave geometrically like her arm. Her arm was fat and curvy. Right in the middle of her shoulder was a triangular indent, like folded paper.

Further down, a disruption ran from the inner elbow through the space between the arm and body and into the hip, where it ended. It was also like a fold, a crease. It folded the flesh of the hip and the air as one piece.

While the woman sat straight in front of me as if I were standing in the room, the floor she sat on was tilted, as if I was above it looking down. The stool's cross stitch of flowers and butterfly was very vivid and densely coloured. The butterfly wings had warm, woollen, stained-glass-window interiors. The only pure white in the picture was inside the wriggled compartments of these wings. Because of this, the butterfly almost seemed to hover off the dirty, used-looking linen of the fabric it was stitched on. It might have risen up into her, sailed through her solid buttock in a way I couldn't understand, or follow.

So this was cubism: you could travel through solid objects and solid objects could travel through you.

Artist's apartment

'I realised that if I'm prepared to ruin a painting, it always works out,' David told us as he drove us up the hill in his black SUV. Isobel, like David, was an artist and doing watercolour paintings. We were going to his apartment in Echo Park to house-sit while he went to visit his girlfriend in San Diego. By the time he came back we'd be on the road, heading towards Arizona.

The apartment backed onto the dry, Australian-looking Elysian Park. It was a low-slung forties complex with peeling concrete and unkempt tropical foliage. The plants seemed to dominate, cracking through and climbing over the concrete. A few guys always seemed to be sitting outside on the garden furniture, talking about the things that interested them, which seemed to be surfing, fishing and driving out to Joshua Tree.

'I found this really nice iridescent beetle,' David said as he opened the front door, pointing to the side. It was sitting, dead, on the top of one of those clear blue plastic barrels of water that you place upside down on your cooler. It was blackish and subtly gleaming.

Inside, the apartment decoration was standard issue: grey carpet with an Ikea rug, the ubiquitous light wood

Ikea furniture, and innocuous stripy cotton cushions on the bed.

David was running late for the train but didn't panic. He packed in an orderly way and left us with some pieces of wild salmon he'd caught in Alaska and smoked himself, and with his cat, Kitty Cat, and drove off to catch the train to San Diego and his girlfriend.

In his living room that evening we discussed David's charmed life, which seemed to consist of fishing and painting. We were envious, because he didn't need to do another job to make ends meet. Making money from painting was giving him plenty of time for fishing. If it hadn't been for the money, it might have been hard to tell which was the serious pursuit and which was the hobby.

David didn't have a television hookup but he did have the whole set of *Blue Planet* DVDs. We watched the one about the creatures of super deep regions and how they live on scales and detritus drifting down from prey eaten closer to the surface. In such utter darkness the sun was still their energy source, coming to them in almost homoeopathic amounts. Some of them were magically illuminated with phosphorescence, others had a lightless existence, never intended to be seen. The cameras lit up one of these fish. It floated just above the ocean floor, mashing its heavy jaw, a picture of obliviousness.

The next morning Isobel went to finish painting a fireplace so that it would look like it was made of marble, and I was left in Echo Park without a car. It was a perfect

LA day. Apparently this perfection happened every day and got monotonous.

I had thought of writing some letters, but instead fussed about stagnantly. I picked up two pennies and a dime off the floor. I folded some of the Arizona maps and campground guides we'd left on the floor trying to work out the best route to Arcosanti.

I felt tired from not sleeping well the night before, and claustrophobic about being in an unfamiliar space. The tide of the apartment was washing right up to my edges, like the spring tides in New Zealand when you would go to the beach and discover no buffer zone of sand to walk on, only sea, the water lapping right up to the stone wall separating beach from back lawns.

I took my little colour portrait of Kevin's guru from the plastic sleeve of my appointment book.

'She's my guru,' he'd said straightforwardly when I first asked about her framed photograph in his bedroom. Since then I'd been to her ashram in upstate New York with him, and he'd bought me this photo. She was in a classic three-quarter thoughtful pose, her chin cupped in her hands. A lipstick red dot sat between her brows. She had a white shawl over an apricot one and a fluffy white knitted skullcap, her black hair curling out from under it. She was like an Indian Princess Diana.

I put my hands up in front of my face, and tried to feel around inside my energy field in the way they'd explained at the ashram. During the exercise in the big auditorium with hundreds of others, I'd thought I *could* feel my energy field and where it stopped and the next thing started. My fingertips had dipped outside of it, like they were dipping into another substance which was cooler, or drier, or smoother. There was something tranquil but foreign about what was beyond, like it was a different gas.

I sat at the table by the window and looked at the greasy spot on the curtain above the futon where I'd slept. Kitty Cat was outside staring at something in the dry, spiky, unsavory-looking grass. It looked like if you walked in it you'd probably step on something unpleasant, something rotten or sharp. Even though David had said to 'make yourself at home and eat anything you like', I tried not to use things up. In the airless kitchen, sealed off from the sun by two polystyrene insulation panels, I used a little peanut butter on another piece of toast. Acting like I was on rations, I saw that there were two toasts' worth of peanut butter left in the jar. 'Take nothing but photographs, leave nothing but footprints,' the signs used to say at the entrances to bush walks in New Zealand. I moved dishes into the kitchen but didn't do them.

In the kitchen a reproduction of one of David's paintings was wedged into the bevelled frame of another painting. It was an invitation to one of his shows, and had the name of his London gallery in acidic yellow on the other side. The image was a pencil drawing overlaid with watercolours, of people going up an escalator. The watercolours were from the fluorescent highlighter palette: yellow and pink mainly. The people were close to faceless. They had the look of people in an architectural artist's impression: blank columns, gliding expressionlessly up and down the angled conveyer belts. He had allowed himself only a light hold on these people. There was no sense of presumption about their inner lives. There was a kind of sanctity, I thought, never too strong, in the way he showed banality and made it seem beautiful and perfect. At the same time a feeling of domination in this scene was accepted deeply and pleasantly.

An actual painting on canvas, a large one, was propped up against drawers near the front door. Like the escalator one, the pencil outlines interlocked with blocks of ethereal fluorescents and grey. People were looking at books in a bookshop. The browsers gathered softly around the shelves, subdued and undynamic.

In David's bathroom above the toilet there was a tooth poster. In the middle of it was a drawing of a giant tooth, cross-sectioned. Nerves like multicoloured ribbons twined and branched in the pulp, the innermost compartment of the tooth. A smaller box to the side held a frontal diagram of the skull of a six-year-old, adult teeth shown as blue pods or capsules floating in the gums above, or below the white milk teeth. Under the tooth chart, butterflies on a butterfly chart were arranged at jaunty angles, floating on the white paper: Papilionidae, Nymphalidae, Pieridae— all shades of yellow.

Back in the main room I opened one drawer to find a fuzzy clot of trout-fishing flies: bodies of pink wool, red feather and iridescent thread mingled together, fitted with exotic tails and headdresses. In fact there was fly-making stuff—microscopic beads and feathers and wool and reels of fine wire and delicate pliers—in all sorts of nooks and crannies in the apartment. Being in this space made me feel like the frog in the 'California Frog Map' on the floor, hopping between vivid things which were collected in little clusters. Some things had an almost electric intensity; the butterflies, the teeth, the fishing flies, and an amazing ornamental shell owl. Others didn't. Did this electricity have something to do with David? There was something here about uniqueness and impersonality, some conflict.

I put my hand into a clear plastic container and picked out one fly. The body of the creature was the brass hook. Its head was the circle of the hook, which a line could be attached to. Its body extended back and turned under like an unhappy dog's tail. From its silver bound and corseted body issued a magnificent spray of soft grey barbs: tiny hairs that could have been taken from the downy part of a feather. It looked like a grey lion with a 'fairy' mane, like the dandelion fairies we used to chase and capture. Once you saw it you ran gleefully to catch it. They were weird to try to capture because they moved so slowly they made a waste of your quickness. You imagined capture as better achieved by floating towards it as if your legs weren't in contact with the ground, your arms closing like a slow sleepy crocodile jaw, but then you would have become like it, and the desire to catch would have evaporated.

On the noticeboard

My lilac board. The field in front of me in my first proper job at the National Library. Padded underneath so pins could be stuck in. It was set into a grey desk unit which was very compact, the shelves that sat about head height casting a gloom onto the working space below. Painted grey mouldings edged the upholstered surface. I didn't pin anything on it. I didn't feel like asserting my individuality; the idea made me feel tired.

Ten years later I again found myself at a grey desk for a few hours a day, in the stationery kiosk at the School of Medicine. I was a temp. The woman who usually worked there had gone on a long holiday. She had made this collage out of glossy cut-out magazine photos of birds taped together. It formed a large brightly coloured sellotapey clump on the noticeboard behind me. I couldn't decide if it was grotesque or beautiful, all those huge vivid birds in a shiny clot. When stock came in, I made black or white knots like corsages with the webbed plastic packing tape and pinned them on the noticeboard too.

Well

The first room in the dungeon is the elevator. It carries you up to work, and for a few seconds each day you're held in there. There is the smell of tremors, there is caramel woodgrain sliding down the walls.

A convex mirror up in the corner shows you yourself looking up. You look a little Alice-like. As if looking through a peephole out at yourself waiting to be let in.

You get 'pulled up' in that elevator like water from a well.

'I didn't pull up Leila—can you hit the elevator?'

'Wait till I pull up Nikki then we'll talk.'

'Meagan's been waiting to be pulled up.'

'Nobody pulled me up.'

Sometimes the lift cannot pull you up, but will not let you out either. Then you press the red emergency button at the top of the control panel. No one is alerted by this; it just makes the door open.

Names

When I was about seven I took to school a pamphlet saying, 'This is to certify that Warren, Elizabeth, John, Derek, Roger and Anna Shortt have changed their name by deed poll and and will now be known as Sanderson.' Or maybe it was something more snappy like 'The Shortts have become Sanderson.' My father was working in an advertising agency at that time and had, I think, got colleagues to word and design the pamphlet. There was something about the wording and design which gave an edge of slickness and lightness, a feeling of copy, rather than plain information. The paper was a thick cream and the lettering a fat brown seventies type.

I gave it to my teacher, Mrs Grayson, and that was that. My surname was changed. I don't remember any reaction from my classmates. I don't remember any strangeness in accepting my new name either, any looking at the new words and inculcating them into my sense of myself. It must have been one those things that don't cause a ripple.

Sometimes I feel a certain inward shamefacedness, almost a giggly feeling, when people ask me if I'm related to this or that Sanderson. I've got to know who some of the real Sandersons are this way. Every now and then I say I'm not related to the actor Martyn Sanderson, who played Frank Sargeson in the film about Janet Frame, and once in a while I say I'm not related to Pippa Sanderson, who apparently is a painter.

When I was working at the medical school, one of my colleagues Maxine and I would tell each other the weird names that came up while we were processing the interloans, names like Coffin and Feijoa.

'Names have energy,' she said. Her married name was Schutte. She told me she liked the energy of it, describing it with her hands in the air. It looked open and fast. What was the energy of Shortt, I wondered? It was also stolid, black and white, clipped. Sanderson was weaker, warmer, and more presentable. Was I now weaker, warmer and more presentable?

Although he says it was because he got called 'Shorty' at school and he didn't want this for his own sons, I still don't fully grasp why my father took this leap.

Knowing how proud and unbending my grandfather Fraser was, I can't believe Dad couldn't foresee his own excommunication from the Shortt family. And yet he went through and did everything, down to the last detail, acting like it was nothing personal.

Is a name important or unimportant? It can't be a particularly powerful thing if you can just cast it off and get a new one. Or, a name might be too powerful: too powerful to live with. Whichever, as an only child, my father made a clean sweep. He made off with the family's future. No more Shortts.

'No, no,' Dad had said in a you've-got-to-be-joking kind of way, when I asked him if his father had visited him when he was in hospital with appendicitis as a child. He had been explaining how in the evenings he'd stood by the window in the brick building at the entrance to the Auckland Domain to see his father drive by on his way home from work. How could a parent drive by their child in hospital? I thought. I had a theory Dad wouldn't have changed our name if he'd liked his father.

'No, he liked Grandad Fraser,' my brother Roger, who dislikes psychobabble, said when I told him my theory. 'Fraser would have visited him, just not every day. Things were different then.' It was hard to find the truth of it. Still, I think of my father watching from the hospital window for his father's car.

Green Tara

My parents and I were driving back from up north and stopped for a coffee in Whangarei, at a shopping complex set alongside a marina. The marina was a tidal estuary, and we walked along a walkway beside it to stretch our legs, triggering tiny crabs to scuttle into their holes in the mud as we went.

We wandered into an art gallery that had been converted from a historic local homestead. In the front area there were painted local scenes and a gift shop with ceramics, glass and jewellery. The main exhibition, *Innerspace II*, was by a Tibetan monk living in Australia. The canvases were bright and intricate, like mandalas, but with contemporary, Western elements too.

One of the images was a bright green bejewelled figure. The title of the painting was *Green Goddess—Mother Tara*. It was a head-and-shoulders portrait and she sat with one hand up in benediction holding a slender plant root. Mother Tara was martian green, and the palm of her hand was red. She wore a highly decorative headdress and mantle, strung with pearls and detailed with yellow and red tiny blossoms and fleurs-de-lys. Two chemical blue lotuses sat on either side of her head, and a golden light emanated from behind her. The background was expressionistic, like a rainbow-coloured splatter painting. The wall text said Mother Tara was the 'supreme creatrix' who had vowed to incarnate only as female.

I hadn't known Tara was an Indian name. I didn't know Mistress Tara's given name, only that she was Jewish. Her 'real' if not original name, the one she'd sign her cheques with, was Ava Montana.

'What do you think of the Den of Iniquity?' I had asked Charles, a houseboy for most of the dungeons around town, when I still worked at The Leg Shoppe, a low-end fetish house. He answered without looking at me. He was never able to look women in the eye and speak directly.

'It's OK . . . it's good, I like it because the headmistress there, Tara, is a female supremacist. She really believes females are superior to males. I like that.' He also said what I had heard from others, that if you were willing to work in quite a regimented environment, you could really learn things, as she had a proper training programme. She even had, apparently, a syllabus: you worked your way through a reading list of key bdsm texts, discussing each book with Tara. After you'd finished the last book, your hourly rate increased.

I had only seen Mistress Tara all decked out once, as Venus at the Roman Goddess party. She was past the daily grind of donning corsets for customers, and was channelling herself into becoming a fetish film star and expanding her business empire. There were a lot of photos and videotapes of her hanging around the dungeon, dressed up in various fetishy guises.

'Remember this is not a democracy,' Tara said at o[ne of]
our staff meetings, after disgruntled discussion about
shift times, 'it's a monarchy.'

The picture of her on the website homepage [was]
typical. She looked like a saloon harlot of the Old W[est.]
There was a red wall, and a stripy chaise longue on w[hich]
she half sat, half reclined. Her hair was in a pinky
chignon. She was wearing a black satin corset with w[hite]
piping. It was not the kind that gives you cleavage, [but]
the shaped kind that trains your bust into a perfect cu[rve.]
Her face had an impenetrable, doll-like expression, [her]
lips were pouted, accentuating her cheekbones. She [was]
leaning back on the chaise longue, but not putting [any]
weight on her behind. You didn't do this as it made y[ou]
look fat. She might have been crossing her legs, wh[ich]
you never actually did, but held one leg lightly touchi[ng]
the one below, so that the flesh didn't smash together a[s it]
did when you relaxed.

Out of uniform she was totally different. I went [to]
stay with her in LA while she was setting up her ne[w]
suburban West Hollywood dungeon. The extra flesh th[at]
she made work so well with corsetry and rubber becam[e]
less formidable in ordinary clothes. She had that of[f]
duty stripper look which was so normal in that city. Sh[e]
walked around in her sweats, carrying a Louis Vuitto[n]
knock-off shoulderbag under her armpit. Her ginger-re[d]
weave looked greasy and itchy. She would scratch it wit[h]
her apricot tips.

Tara didn't want to stand out in public when she didn'[t]
have to. After dressing as a punk all through art school i[n]

the eighties, she'd told me, she realised at some point that you can be more radical if you do things unobtrusively. Then, the less her radicality expressed itself in her clothing, the more it bred under wraps. 'Choose your battles': a fundamental tenet from her favourite book, *The 48 Laws of Power*.

Tara's face had the nipped, stripped look that comes from getting work done. Her nose was very neat, and she'd got rid of the veins that make dark rings under eyes. I had been fairly uneducated about 'beauty'. The extent of my regime before coming into this industry was to pluck the hairs between my eyebrows, making them fully separate.

Tara was encouraging me to become more highly polished. First it was the nails she suggested needed doing, then facials, next eyebrow waxing, upper lip waxing, and so it went on. Weaves and falls were very inexpensive in LA, she hinted. I resisted, thinking I couldn't afford to get all this stuff done. It also seemed like it created a lot of extra work: once you're well maintained, you are always in a comparative state of disrepair.

On yet another appointmentless afternoon at the house, we went to get our nails done at the local shopping centre. Pink Nails had a neon sign in the window of this featureless one-level complex. There were eight or ten women working in there, each with a small bureau covered in equipment and supplies: brushes, cuticle clippers, the little resting pad you put your hand on, a magnifying light, the wooden sticks which cotton balls were attached to, files.

The women greeted Tara with familiarity. She said she'd brought her friend Michelle from New York and was going to leave her here while she went away for an hour. I needed a manicure/pedicure and Tara wanted me to get tips. She spoke for me.

'She wants *natural*-coloured tips,' she explained in an italicised way.

'Yes,' they said, 'we'll give you a very *natural* look.' They were humouring me.

We sat down and waited. Tara and I looked through the *People* magazines. There was a portrait of Demi Moore on the cover, looking stellar at forty.

'Let's tear her apart,' Tara said, poring closer. She turned to the bikini shots, commenting on how wrong she looked in her gym-enhanced body, and how bad it was for a person not to have enough body fat. Then she went to buy a washer-dryer, and I had my tips put on.

The woman who did my nails did not have an American name like the women in the Korean nail salons did in New York. Consequently, I didn't catch it. She was the sought-after acrylic tips and silk wrap craftsperson though, because she made the tips thin, which is something you can never get the New York manicurists to do.

'It's a battle,' Tara warned me. 'You have to say to them over and over again, *not too thick!* No, *thinner!*', as the thicker they are, the more obtrusive the gap between the cuticle and the beginning of the plastic as the nail grows, so you have to go back for fills.

My nail technician's inexpensive clothing seemed elegant on her. Her dark glassy hair was up in one of those plastic hinging combs, and she wore a lime green T-shirt. She chopped down bits of bright white plastic and stuck them on my nails, took a brush and dipped it in a pretty pinkish powder, then in some liquid, then rolled the filler on in a glob, smoothing deftly. The salon smelt like a boat building workshop.

'Do you wear some kind of filtration mask?' I asked. She gave a vague answer. It seemed she was used to the smell. She asked me about New York and 9/11. I gave a heartfelt stock answer. I asked her where she was from. She said she had come from Vietnam fourteen years ago and she was thirty-five now. She would have been eight when the war ended. Now she worked in a nail salon, and it was Veterans Day, as it happened. She seemed like one of those beautiful girls with smooth surfaces to whom nothing can adhere.

Tara came back eventually; she hadn't found the right washing machine. I went back to wait with the *People* magazines while Tara had one broken tip repaired. I looked at my new nails. They weren't all that long, and sort of a whitey-pinky colour. I could see my old nail growing, curved and a dirtier hue, in behind the thicker white fake. They looked odd with my falling-apart T-shirt and trousers.

My mother had preferred short nails. I remember her using the word 'claws' to describe how long nails looked. She would keep hers just a few millimetres long, and curved. She had a metal nail file as long as a chopstick, which she never lost and still has. It ate up your nails, leaving little powdery flaps still attached. She also used to push her cuticles back, bravely, I thought, because it always made me feel faint to try to push my own back.

Her hands were different from mine. They were bigger boned and stronger. If I couldn't get the lid off a jar, she would always be able to do it. The nails were big and flat and round, and her fingers were quite thick and blunt, like the hands of those thick-limbed, heavy-lidded Picasso women running on the beach. In cold weather, or sometimes even in the summer, my mother's fingers would turn completely white. She'd immerse them in warm water to get the blood to come back.

My father had nice hands. His fingers were reasonably long, and his fingernails deep bedded and well proportioned. There was never a loose roughness to his hands, always a self-consciousness. When he was about to sign something he would clasp his pen and hold it a centimetre or two above the paper. It would hover there, poised and moving as if in trepidation at the dive. He pressed hard when signing, almost attacking the paper. The signature was full of jerks and abrupt angles.

Oddly enough, because he did virtually nothing domestic, my father cut my nails until I left home at nineteen. Somehow there was no such thing as nail clippers in our household and so I needed someone to cut my left hand. We would stand at the window of his bedroom, leaning on the white sill, with, directly in front of us the cherry tree which in springtime bloomed pink and attracted tui. Dad would stand on my right-hand side with his quality Swedish nail scissors, and hold each finger quite tightly as he cut it. He had a slightly doddery imprecision. He would purse his lips in concentration, and then run his thumb over the newly cut edge as if to feel for burrs or rough spots after each nail had been cut. The nails would drop down two storeys to the concrete below.

A red brick church

'Well, I think it's horses for courses,' Dad said in a moderating voice, at the end of my diatribe against people who buy churches and convert them for private living. Tony and I had come up to Auckland for Christmas. It was early evening and we all had a drink. I was leaning at one end of the kitchen by the light switches with my sparkling water. Dad was leaning against the bench at the window end of the kitchen. My mother and Tony were opposite each other across the width of the room.

We'd been listening to Dad while he held forth about the gay thing having hijacked a perfectly good girl's name. No one would be able to call their daughter Gay now, he said, and that was a shame.

'I don't even think about that with Gay Tremain,' Mum said. Next Dad started to get excited about how good the Taranaki Savings Bank was, telling me I should open an account there. He is all for smaller businesses who take on the big boys.

I worried that the tendency to get exercised over trivia was a family trait. I remembered when the crockery had rattled on my grandparents' dark polished dining table as my Grandad Fraser's fist had slammed down onto it during a family dinner.

'*Gitaway! Gitaway!*' He bellowed his outrage at a package tour company that would take such liberties with the English language.

Although it was hard to argue with 'horses for courses', the private ownership of churches did provoke me. Who is anyone to buy a church?

We were not a religious family. I had never noticed my father displaying any religious feeling. We had gone into a small brick church a few months earlier in Matakohe. It was empty, and open for inspection or worship. I sat down in one of the pews. It wasn't an elaborate church, but it had a suffused illuminating light, and was distinguished by its lovely lectern at the front, carved with Maori motifs. Dad stood at the altar area and made loud observations about the architecture. It could have been a bank or a train station he was looking at.

My mother had more reverence. Sometimes something would cause her to be overcome by the same kind of hard-to-interpret joy as the female character that looks out of the window and sees the pears in Katherine Mansfield's 'Bliss'. I bought her that book once, thinking she might recognise herself.

She's not religious either though. She's always been frosty about the church. They had made up my grandfather so he didn't look like himself, she said, when he was lying in his coffin.

I was four, and don't remember seeing him in there. I could imagine him lying there, twinkly, with a hint of blue around his eyes. But maybe it wasn't like that. Maybe he looked hollowed and the make-up was pancaked on and obscured his skin. I spent the burial at my mother's thighs anyway as, way up above, she cried. Just as she hadn't forgiven the funereal make-up artist, she was also still angry at someone who'd attempted to console her by saying Grandad was better off where he'd gone.

My brother Daniel shares these feelings about organised religion, even though, like me, he has had only the lightest of brushes with it. In his poem 'Where is God?' he finds God in a whole list of places, 'But,' he declares in the last line, 'I've never found God in a church.'

Sometimes when there was nothing much to do in my department at the medical school, I would get sick of trying to look busy and go for a walk round the hospital corridors, ending up at the Fuel coffee cart.

One day I walked in front of a man wheeling himself in the hospital front doors.

'Cold today!' an elderly couple said to him as the wind blew in with him. The stitch lines on his leg stumps had dried blood on them. How strange to have the wind whistling around your fresh stumps. They looked spongy, the flesh grey yellow. Well stuffed and sewn. The elderly woman rubbed the back of her husband's neck and put up the collar of his windbreaker.

I walked into the prayer chapel down the hallway. I wondered if I should be in there since I wasn't grieving or worshipping, but no one else was there anyway. As soon as I went inside, the business of the corridor receded. The door was screened off with a chrome hospital partition on wheels, which had cream linen stretched between its panels. The voices from the corridor floated through it. I leaned back in one of the dark green chairs and put my feet on the one in front, listening to them.

The clop of heels on lino, high and low, a wheeze, a yip, the squeal of doors, the swish of trousers, the high ding of the lifts, whistling, rhythms tapped out on thighs, pens clicking maniacally, the feeble smooth drawing back sound of the automated doors. Snippets of interaction.

'You right, Don?'

'Yeah, yeah.'

'The chapel's there to the right,' a modulated female voice. The smell of toast.

I was aware that at any moment someone might come in. I leaned my head against the cold concrete wall. There was a sound like the building breathing, like bellows, gulping and expelling. I thought it must have been the automatic doors, the constantly moving entrance to the hospital. Then I realised it was the lifts, moving up and down the liftwell. It was tireless, like water moving.

'Isn't it amazing that this goes on every second, when we're not here too? This constant churning?' my mother had said as we stood above the Huka Falls, watching.

I willed this spartan, un-aesthetic space to be tender and illuminating. The walls were pale pink. There was a Jesus and Madonna up the front of the space. They had rosy flesh. The Madonna had bright blue eyeshadow.

74

They sat up there with a piano and a gilt-edged bible. A gold-rimmed clock made a rhythmic, precise tick. Each tick was like two notes struck almost together but not quite.

There was a watery picture across the narrow chapel space. A coastal rock pool scene. It was a highly skilled depiction. You could see the underwater rockscape through a surface of glassy, blue green water. My eyes kept wandering into this enchanted shallow water. Everything was more precisely rendered, more serene, more refreshed in there, protected from what swirled around in the atmosphere above.

One young man came in. Luckily I had already taken my feet off the seat. I had seen him around. He was a registrar, and he looked like a frightened rabbit. I couldn't tell if he thought I was invading his privacy or he was invading mine. He prayed Muslim prayers. I supposed he must come in a few times a day. I averted my eyes. Did this little chapel prefer the Muslim registrar to me, as he was worshipping, and I was just sitting back, looking? Was I welcome here? In a place like this, I reassured myself, one is always welcome. That's the beauty of it.

For several months I walked to the medical school in Newtown each day from the Aro Valley. Somehow, rather than being invigorating, that particular route through the city usually felt mildly harrowing. I would walk down through Aro Park, past the funeral home and the shrunken fruit in boxes outside the Shalimar dairy and into upper Willis Street, opposite the hotel with mirror windows that I tried not to look at myself in, against a tide of people walking into the city. Opposite, on Hunter's corner, a new block of apartments stood, with black grilles suggesting juliet balconies. Apparently there had been a Catholic church there once but it had burnt down.

The intersection would be frenetic with car activity. A three-lane flow of traffic streamed one way down upper Willis Street, periodically interrupted by a stream coming off Webb Street. There is rarely a break in these alternating flows, but when there is, people get sick of waiting for the cross signal and try to dash across.

During my first days of rushing late to work I encountered the sobering squeal, thud, and strange silence of a car hitting a body. I came to the corner and saw a raincoated figure lying inert on the wet grey asphalt. People had already rushed over and put the person in the recovery position.

Along Webb Street amongst apartment blocks, both new and under construction, car yards, panelbeaters and the odd derelict bungalow, there were also two churches and a synagogue. A modern three-storey chalet with a cherry tree blossoming out the front had a painted sign which said 'The Church of Christ meets here—You are very welcome!' A bit further down on the other side, parents would be dropping off small children at the Moriah School and Kindergarten with its blue pentacle and glass pyramid, through which the sun always seemed to be held and glowing at ten past eight in the morning.

A block down there was the Wellington Central Church. A large blue painted panel, in keeping with the area's commercial tone, signalled its presence. There is no religious imagery or symbolism on the sign; it simply carried the byline 'In partnership with the Apostolic Church Movement of New Zealand'. Other traditional church buildings which used to be in the street had either been replaced by apartment buildings as with Hunter's corner, or retained and converted into apartments. About halfway down the street, an old red brick church with gates, carports and new rooms pushing through its roofline, was clearly now residential.

I wondered what denomination this church had been, so I looked it up on the internet. There were two undated photographs in the National Library collection captioned 'Catholic Apostolic Church'. I couldn't make out the writing on the sign outside the front door, which must have named the church, minister and service times.

In the exterior view, this simple pitch-roofed brick structure was set in a treeless yard. There wasn't a single tree in sight beyond the property either, only the tentacle of a climber on the left-hand fence. A low, stepped brick wall separated the empty yard from the footpath.

It stood, solid and squat but upward-pointing in its parched environment. The roof was tiled, and painted white concrete trimmed the brick. There were some decorative features: a rose window, small slitted windows, and what looked to me like miniature turrets, made from cast concrete.

I printed these images out and took them to the Catholic Archives to see if they had more information.

At the Catholic Archives in Hill Street, Sister de Porres shook my hand as if I had come into her home, and brought me coffee on a coaster with cute insects which said 'millennium bugs'.

She brought me a file but it turned out to be on the church that had burnt down on Hunter's corner. The archive didn't have any information on the red brick church.

'I don't think the Catholic Apostolic Church is a *Roman* Catholic church,' she said.

She put her greyish finger on the photocopy I had of the interior and ran it over the altar area.

'It definitely *looks* like a Catholic church inside. This whole area is the sanctuary; it has the lamps. Catholic churches always have a lamp over the tabernacle. The tabernacle is where the host is kept, and there are the rails.'

'So that's the sanctuary, this whole bit at the front?' I asked, writing 'sanctuary' on the photocopy.

'You're not a Catholic then . . .'

'No,' I answered apologetically.

'No no, that's all right,' she said, as if to reassure me it was still OK to be using the Catholic Archives. 'No, I didn't think you were a Catholic. How were you brought up?'

'Kind of as nothing,' I said. 'My parents were pretty secular, and I think their parents were too. They made us go to church a few times so we would know what it was like.'

'Oh, yes. I always ask,' she said.

I looked back at the photocopy. The interior of the

church was really quite simple and almost perfectly symmetrical down to the two identical vases of flowers flanking the tabernacle. The ceiling was held up with heavy wooden trusses, dark against white panels, and there was plain glass in the windows. There was a wooden floor and carpet running up the central aisle dividing two banks of wooden pews. As Sister de Porres said, everything was Catholic except there was no statue at the front. Usually there would be a Holy Mother, or a St Joseph, I think she said. In fact, there were no images at all adorning the interior.

That there was a church she didn't know about sparked the Sister's interest and she went off to look it up, coming back with a green-bound *Encyclopaedia of Religion*. The entry under 'Catholic Apostolic Church' said it had been started in England in 1826, with a small prayer circle who believed that the reestablishment of the primitive church with its twelve apostles was the groundwork that had to be laid for the second coming. A man called Edward Irving even set the second coming at the specific date of 1864. In 1835 twelve men spent a year in prayer then left England for mission spots around the globe.

It was hard to find out much at all about the Catholic Apostolics who had inhabited the red brick church. I found reference to them in *A History of the Charismatic Movements in New Zealand*, and in a small pamphlet which contained the first three sermons of the church. These were given when the congregation was still in its first building, the old wooden St Peter's the Apostolics had bought from the Anglicans down the road.

'Three Sermons,' the pamphlet read, 'Preached in the Catholic Apostolic Church, Webb Street, Wellington, New Zealand, on its being opened for Divine Service, November 1880.' No preacher's name was given. The titles of the sermons were equally long-winded, for example: 'The Unity of the Church of Christ, broken by schism and its restoration by apostles'. They went on, the page filled with typefaces.

By the time they were given, November 1880, the critical date of 1864 had long come and gone.

'The apostles did their work zealously,' the unnamed preacher said of his church, 'building up those who received their testimony into congregations in every Christian country to which they had access. And now their work is done and they have all been taken to their rest except one. As I said before, their work according to man's judgment is a failure, for the baptised nations have rejected them, even as the Jews rejected the Lord and his first apostles.'

But, he added, 'He will yet justify them and their work.' The sect simply had to wait for the sign of their selection by God as firstfruits of the harvest, because according to Isaiah:

With stammering lips and another tongue He will speak to his people.

In *A History of the Charismatic Movements in New Zealand*, James E. Worsfold describes the Apostolics' end:

They would appear to have overemphasised the near return of Christ, thereby obscuring the continuing purpose of God in the church on earth. When the signs foretold to precede this great event did not in the fulness appear, a mild form of confusion affected many of their number and in an excellent spirit of submission the church went [. . .] 'from motivation to meditation'.

It took a long time for the church to die.

Worsfold reveals that it was already 1928 when in optimistic spirit '. . . a red, brick church of handsome Gothic design and seating for 120 was erected . . .'.

It was about 1960 when the church was finally passed into the hands of the Anglicans.

Next time I was walking past I stopped and had a look at the apartments. I didn't know how much time had passed since it had functioned as a 'house of God'. The place seemed crisp and stately behind a grey remote-operated gate. Ivy was growing on the bricks. A Range Rover and a BMW were parked under the carports which were newly built with eaves to echo the church's roof line. A bright green Tommy's Real Estate sign was still up, advertising one of the apartments for sale.

I walked further down to the Wellington Central Church which worked 'In partnership with the Apostolic Church Movement of New Zealand' to see if they were some kind of offshoot of the Catholic Apostolic Church.

They were on the ground floor of an office block on the corner of Webb and Torrens Streets. The office building was six storeys of pebbly orange panels and mirror glass forming an unmemorable shape. The Consumer's Institute appeared to occupy much of the building and one of their banners was positioned right above the Church's sign. 'Make a dent in your car insurance' it read.

I was looking in the window for service times when a young man opened the door and asked if I needed any help. He was round faced and had an Eastern European accent.

'This is a completely new Apostolic church,' he told me when I asked him if this place had moved from the old brick building up the road. 'It's a Protestant church. I think they came from Paraparam.'

I asked if I could sit down for a little while. It was not a conventionally contemplative space. It was low ceilinged, clad with typical office materials and lit with fluorescent tubes. At the far end, the stage was set with a drum kit, synthesiser and large speakers. The only religious images were a couple of weak paintings with the words *light* and *Lord* brushed on them. There were a few young men about, busy with cleaning or shifting gear.

I gathered pamphlets about prayer and rock and missions off the display table. At the back there was a prayer board. I could have taken home a laminated picture-magnet of a young New Zealand woman teaching in Japan, to stick on the fridge and remember in my prayers. To not be swayed by the Shinto/Buddhist atmosphere in Japan and stay strong in God, was one of her requests.

I decided to call up one of the two real estate agents listed on the Tommy's sign to ask if I could have a look inside the apartment for sale. I left a message with Bill Mathieson's message service the next day, and he called back five minutes later.

'That was fast,' I said, surprised.

'I like to be fast,' he said. After I said I wasn't a potential buyer but a writer, he was still accommodating, and agreed to show me the apartment the next day.

'At least you look like a client,' he said as we walked into what would have been the side entrance to the main chapel. I was surprised at this as I felt kind of scrappy. I was at the stage of pregnancy where I really needed to get some different clothes but hadn't got round to it, so I had my elasticated trousers turned down at the waist, and my shoes were coming apart. I had felt conscious of our messy station wagon too, and had hoped he wouldn't see me in it when I was parking. He had pulled up in a shiny black car.

There was something dynamic and masculine about him, like he'd just got out of the shower and slapped on some aftershave. He had a blunt face, dark blond hair that was longer at the front and slicked back with product. Half a gold front tooth glinted in his mouth, and he had on a long, expensive-looking woollen coat. He gave the feeling of a bullish sexuality somehow contained.

When we opened the door there were two lithe brown cats prowling around. As he got out his colour pamphlets advertising the place, they jumped up on the bench and wanted to be patted. I stroked the cats with enthusiasm.

The apartment belonged to a professional couple, Mathieson told me. It took up a sixth of the church, inside its right shoulder. The space that would once have been the front of the nave and risen clear up to the trusses had been divided into three levels of living space. The newly constructed interior walls created cosy spaces, and the cream carpet and paint created an insulated effect. The spaces were so domestically scaled that for moments I'd forget I was in a former church, until coming across some heavy fixture that hadn't been covered up.

A narrow staircase led up to a mezzanine-level sunroom in which a giant wooden truss poked through an ill-fitting hole made in beige carpet, and on up through the ceiling. The room was empty except for a sofa, a few magazines and a metallic blue pilates ball.

Where the kitchen was, with its sleek stainless-steel fittings, would once have been outside. The former outside wall divided the kitchen from the living room, which now contained a stereo and a décor-enhancing burgundy painting with text on it. Parishioners would once have sat there in wooden pews, with the hymns and psalms numbered on the tablet in front of them.

Mathieson said that many interested parties found the idea of living in a former church unproblematic, although some were completely turned off by it. He told me that Peter Johnstone, who also lived in the complex, was the developer, but he was not able to remember the name of the architectural firm that designed the conversion. I had thought all that stuff would have been part of the spiel, but perhaps the people buying apartments in churches weren't interested in these details.

I asked him if he liked being a real estate agent.

'It's like being a celebrity without being famous,' he said, describing how you could never get a rest from people. It peeved him too, that people he met socially always wanted to talk about the market. As with rugby in this country, everyone was an armchair authority.

'New Zealanders have an unhealthy obsession with real estate,' he judged.

'God, it's so tidy. I suppose that's just for selling . . .' I said as we shut the door on the immaculate apartment.

'Professional couple,' he said, as if this was normal for professional couples. He proceeded to talk about some people's houses he went into, and how he couldn't believe they couldn't just put a load of washing through. Being one of these people, I thought about trying to defend them, but we were nearing the gates. I thanked him again for his time. He said it was fine, and that it's always good to get out and do things, as something always comes of keeping moving.

'You've had quite a lot of insight into the real estate business today,' he said, referring to the insight he had given into his own feelings.

'A hundred per cent more than I had before,' I replied, off the mark.

At Romulus Consulting Group, Director Peter Johnstone was all in black and needing to go to a funeral. I said I was sorry, wondering if I should be there at all, but he waved that off; he was paying his respects to a friend of his mother's. He was a smoothly mannered and smoothly dressed man in his sixties, with grey hair and a network of fine blood vessels webbing his cheeks and nose.

Romulus Consulting Group had a tight-knit floor plan. I had walked in a few minutes early, thinking that a receptionist would give me somewhere to wait. She placed me in the thick of the small, open-plan office, at a little round table.

The office was filled with younger men, dressed neat-casual. The one directly in front of me had pictures of mountain bikes stuck up on his office partition. The director was set apart by his age, and by the distinctive wooden desk he sat at. His view was out across the motorway which runs behind The Terrace and to a row of large wooden homes sitting precariously on the other side of the gully. The windows were steamed up.

I was within eyeshot of Johnstone, wedged in a thoroughfare, and people had to squeeze past me to get to him.

I tried to think about the name Romulus. I knew it was to do with founding Rome, being raised by wolves, and that there was also Remus. I thought of a full shiny row of bronze teats on a sculpture, exquisitely lit against a light grey seamless backdrop. An artefact in a museum, I had a postcard of it at home. Her three young rode on her back above her protruding ribcage. She had a lion's body with a squirrel's tail and a human face. The face had close-cropped human hair, devil's ears, and a stricken expression with lines of age around the eyebrows.

I got out my little dictaphone as Johnstone sat down at the table, explaining I wouldn't necessarily use these recordings; it was just that if I needed to quote him, I could do it accurately. He gave a gentle laughing snort as I said 'quote you'. I wasn't sure if he was laughing with me, or at me, or at himself.

I had a neat list of questions written in small green

printing in my exercise notebook, all of which were answered efficiently. Peter had bought the church because it was a great space and had a nice feeling about it. He'd converted it into six residences, and now lived in one of them. There had been a lot of plans drawn up by the architects. The architects had had vested interests in their own plans for the space because they too had wanted to live there, he said. Johnstone had eventually gone back to his first ideas about how to divide up the space. We got to the end of my questions very quickly, without any surprises. I wondered if he saw the last question, which I was too intimidated to ask: 'Why the gate?'

I had thought to myself as I'd walked past, why do they need more protection than anyone else on the street? I thought of the low concrete wall in the National Library photograph, and how you could have stepped over it without much effort. The apartments were more cloistered than a church.

I'd read an article in the *Listener* which said that gated communities were becoming blockages for emergency services. They have their own streets inside which connect to the streets on the outside, but non-residents can't drive through them. What if someone has a heart attack in there and the ambulance can't get in? the article asked. Councils, having somehow forgotten to think about whether or not gated communities should be regulated, were now concerned that permeability was being lost. From the outside the communities represented a dead zone.

Although the apartment complex wasn't a gated

community, this was something like my feeling when I walked past and noticed it was no longer a church. Once open, now closed. It was like a mutated cell, in a way. But sitting there in Peter Johnstone's office, in the logic of his world, the question wilted.

We said our goodbyes, and he left hurriedly, clutching a tie, as I collected up my papers. He kindly promised further help if I needed it and gave me a contact for Father Ambrose of the Russian Orthodox Church which had last occupied the building, and made photocopies of the architect's floor plans. Just as we'd consigned each other to the past, we met again going down in the lift. With tie now on, he introduced me to one of his business partners.

I ended up walking down The Terrace with this man, who told me that there had been a lot of journalists and researchers contacting the company these days, probably because they had engineered some high profile projects, like the new Catholic church near the Mt Victoria tunnel. We jointly admired its fish motif patterning. He said what was good about it was that it was an honest building, that there were no 'hidden workings'.

'He likes to scare people with his cape,' Peter Johnstone had said of Father Ambrose, who apparently still lived near the apartments. I thought while I was on a roll I might as well knock on his door and see if he could give me a clear idea of the history of the building, since no one else had been able to.

The house beside the apartments had a xeroxed sign

taped to the patio with the street number on it. It had a decrepit façade with bits of wood missing from it. There were dingy curtains on both the windows. A whole line of dusty stuffed toys were lined up along one ledge, peering out at the street. When I looked closer I saw there was another line behind them. There was a stained-glass sticker of an Orthodox cross on the window too, and next to the buzzer some writing in what I thought was Russian and a small diagrammatic drawing of a cross and a skull. These things were Gothic as in the subculture: at once macabre and cute. I knocked on the door a couple of times, but there was no response. I hadn't really expected one, I realised.

Barry Lonergan, partner in Dickson Lonergan Architects, was practically my neighbour, it turned out. If I stood on our path I could see his French doors. Dickson Lonergan had designed the conversion of the Webb Street church into apartments. Their website listed church architecture as an area of expertise. It had pictures of work they'd done: in Hawera, a church with stark white crosses and full columns on the outside, while inside there were white walls and polished wood floors like a gallery; and in Palmerston North a modern 'gathering area' attached to an historic church. The Webb Street conversion wasn't displayed.

I walked down our path on a weekday morning to visit Lonergan. He'd had an accident he was still recovering from, so I was to call in the morning to check, because some days he still didn't feel up to doing much. He was a small man in in his fifties I guessed, with soft grey hair. He was wearing jeans and a long-sleeved T-shirt. His home was one half of a semi-detached building. The ground level was a largely white open-plan interior with black leather furniture. The French doors opened out onto decking and wet Aro Valley foliage.

Lonergan went to make a cup of tea, and I was just sitting down, when sounds of mild dismay came from the kitchen. Someone had left the plug in the tub of the washing machine, he reported. I went through. There was water seeping from the laundry and creeping rapidly across the pale vinyl of the kitchen floor. The architect was standing in a little pantry space with the water coming around the corner, keeping it away from the cupboards, looking a bit indecisive. He threw a set of camel-coloured bedsheets down to soak up some of the flood. I said if he had a mop I could stem the flow from my end.

We spent the next ten minutes in partial silence, pushing the tide back. I was absorbing small amounts into the mop sponge and squeezing it into a bucket.

'A good way to clean the kitchen floor,' I said. 'Not that it was dirty.'

Finally the washing machine stopped pumping out water, and we'd collected the worst of it. We left the damp floor, went back to the leather chairs, and Lonergan began to talk about the church apartments, getting up occasionally when sitting down became too uncomfortable.

He didn't know anything about when the church was built or who built it, and he didn't really rate it architecturally. He thought it 'fundamentally wasn't a particularly fine example of ecclesiastical architecture'. This had led to some of his differences with Peter Johnstone, as he didn't think it was that important to keep the integrity of the building intact, and had wanted to build more extensively out from the brick shell rather than regard that as a boundary. There were a lot of ventilation problems with living spaces constructed inside a space with windows that don't open, he explained.

I asked him if he could say what it was that made the architecture not exemplary.

'Well, it's just a basic example of a church,' he said. 'If it was, say, part of that community, and a strong focal point of what was the Te Aro community, then it would have quite strong meaning in social terms, but it was a place where the Russian Orthodox people came to practise their faith from anywhere in Wellington. It could have been anywhere.

'They took out all their religious symbols, and once you take all that stuff out, all you've got really is some coloured-glass windows and a space.'

'What would be the style?' I asked. 'Is it Gothic, or is it a bit of a mishmash?'

'Well, it's a bit of a mishmash, I don't know, what do you call it—' he searched, '—neo-Gothic.'

He agreed with me that the Webb Street area was in transition to being primarily apartments. I asked him what his views on gentrification were. He thought if you were shrewd enough and 'that's what your game was' you bought where the students were.

'There's a difference now,' he pointed out, 'because

they're building purpose-made apartments for students, and I don't know what effect that'll have on gentrification. I wonder if that process will still take place because of the large amount of low-cost housing that's now being built. In the end they might become slum-type areas.'

I called Lonergan up again later, to ask if he thought it would be OK for me to contact the osteopath he'd told me he knew in the building. He said, yes, he thought that would be fine, and that he was an articulate and interesting man who'd probably have something to say. He mentioned something about being at home because of his accident. I asked him if he'd tried osteopathy.

'Oh, I've tried everything—spiritual healers in Brazil—there's not much I haven't tried,' he said.

'Would you live in a converted church?' I asked Peter McLeavey. I had been looking at his William Dunning show: granite grey drawings of seated men flanking sarcophagi. Each of the drawings was the same arrangement, with the figures set in front of a wood of leafless trees. On the left was always an important Maori man such as Tahupotiki Ratana, on the right always an important Pakeha man, like Samuel Marsden. The sarcophagi contained images of related architecture: the round Ratana church building, for example.

There was something I liked very much about the drawings; it was something right inside them that I couldn't articulate. It was a cranky project, making those very symmetrical codifications about people and history.

It was a mind that couldn't allow mess, which would seem to be a limitation. There was a lack of elegance, through trying to force the unruliness of past events into a repeating formula. But the stiffness and awkwardness with which these figures sat within the spheres of Dunning's conception was the beauty. Dunning didn't just ask questions, he tried to answer them.

Peter sat on his upright chair with a red watch on his wrist.

'A nice space is a nice space,' he said, affirming that, yes, he would be happy to live in a converted church. I felt a certain disappointment at this. And confused. I supposed I was a conservative young idealist. Perhaps I was a crank like William Dunning.

'See you at eleven and we'll have coffee for you,' said Graham Redding. Redding was a minister at the Presbyterian church of St John's in the City, who had recently written a paper titled 'Reflections on storied place as a category for exploring the significance of the built environment'. I had made an appointment to talk to him about a theological view of sacred space.

St John's was on Willis Street, not far from my house, so I bought some madeleines on the way and walked down to the church. When I entered the main office, which was a large, contemporary building on the church grounds, a woman with short, sleep-rumpled hair slid open a glass window, and told me she'd let me through. She smiled through from the other side as I pulled the door and it stayed tightly shut. After a few seconds of delay the magnetic lock on the glass door released, and she took me to his office.

Somewhere in his late forties I judged, Redding was tall and olive skinned with long features: a long face, and long legs and hands. He wore a standard, light blue business shirt. His office was spacious and orderly. I felt he would know where a thing was if he needed to find it. There was a big desk in the middle and a few stiff padded chairs around a hexagonal coffee table. The main feature of the room was a white bookcase built in along the entire left-hand wall. The minister asked the woman with rumpled hair to make us coffee, and when she brought it in she spilled some on the carpet. He cleaned it up with tissues.

Redding spoke very fluently straight off, with relevance to my question about whether or not the Webb Street building was a sacred space. His voice was loud and clear, and he did not search around for words. Whenever I butted in to formulate a question I was aware that my more nebulous, grasping way of thinking was altering the pace he had set. I had an awareness of pushing my thoughts above the coffee table where they hovered, more like statements, containing different emotions. As I asked these cloudy questions he kept tuning his answers towards the point on the continuum of the Presbyterian position on the sacred—some point between people and a place.

'What my paper explores,' he explained, 'is a more relational or dynamic view of what constitutes sacred space. It's not so much that a space is set aside as sacred in some kind of magical way, but rather it's very much linked with the community. That means when those ingredients are dispersed, by their very nature a place is no longer sacred in the same kind of way. It might still have connotations, and might still have certain memories and a legacy of what it once was, but we mustn't operate in a superstitious way.'

'To give an example,' he continued, 'at various times in my ministry I might be called in to a retirement home where someone's died, and the nursing staff want me to have some prayer because the dead person's been in this room; they want it cleansed, as it were, to be made ready for another person. I might go in and "cleanse" one room, but a different set of nursing staff might not deem it necessary so I don't do it for another room when a person dies. Does that mean that one room is somehow more sanctified and more holy than the room next to it that didn't have that prayer? I would say no.'

Blessedness did not exist independently of us, he seemed to be saying. I'd once been at an energy healing workshop where we were shown a book of microscopic photographs of ice from different rivers. Some of the rivers had ice that formed beautifully intact snowflake-like patterns. Others were disrupted and murky. The rivers in untouched or sacred places tended to exhibit the most splendid patterns. The Hudson in New York where we were was kind of okay. The Thames in London was the absolute worst. Our teacher had also shown us another picture of a piece of bread that was just sitting there, and then the piece of bread when it had been blessed. The blessed bread was sitting in a fug of light.

'When I do some of those rituals,' Redding continued,

'I'm doing it more for the psychological reasons of those that are involved, rather than an inherent belief that this space needs to be cleansed or made holy in some way.'

He explained how the same principles applied to the Eucharist.

'It's not that these elements literally become the body and blood of Christ (and therefore as an officiating minister I have to consume it at the end). If the people are gathered to partake of the elements, they become for them, by faith, the body and blood of Christ. But at the end of the communion service we say that because the community is no longer gathered and the ritual has ended, these are just bread and wine at the end of the day.'

I supposed as long as we could isolate something in our minds, we were always performing our own little consecrations and deconsecrations of things.

'What say you're in a café and a man puts his hand on yours and you don't want it there?' a visiting lecturer for Metaphysics 101 had asked us years ago. He was a Texan with a huge golden moustache.

If you didn't want to tell him to take it off, you had to disown your hand, actually abandon it there on the table under his. This was bad faith, apparently.

Graham Redding thought an unbending attitude towards sanctified space could be 'unhelpful'. He pointed to the contested territory of Israel and Palestine.

'You've got competing claims about what is sacred,' he said. 'Whose view of what is sacred should prevail? I would dare to suggest that the conflict in the Holy Land is the most unholy of conflicts and has been for generations.

Surely,' he said, 'the presence of conflict, hatred, revenge and genocide has desanctified the so-called Holy Land, where so much innocent blood has been spilt.'

I asked him how he had come to be a minister. He had trained as an accountant, he told me, which provided an income but didn't 'expand the mind'. So, while most of his friends were doing their OE, Redding stayed at university and completed a theology degree.

'This must be the perfect job,' I commented, thinking of the combination of expanding the mind and helping people. He said in many ways it was, but he also felt the burden of needing to keep numbers up, hence the billboards which imitate the Tui beer 'Yeah right' campaign.

I had often walked past these little bits of religious humour, posted outside the church. One had said, 'It doesn't matter what you believe, just so long as you're sincere.' Then, the negation, 'Yeah right.' I hadn't got it. The Tui ads worked by stating an idea that the general population is supposed to think is crazy, and then deflating it with a withering 'Yeah right'. But the statement here was not obviously crazy to me. It doesn't matter what you believe, just so long as you're sincere. The more I thought about it, the more complex it seemed, which was the opposite of the Tui ads. The subtle thing, the inverse sting of this spoof, was that it was not at all populist, not obvious, had no clear punchline, and even if you thought you saw one, it wasn't very funny. I liked that.

'The key to happiness? Self-esteem, self-belief, self-improvement, self-expression, self-fulfillment . . .' This was the current preface to 'Yeah right', which I did get.

The St John's logo sat underneath the overused but widely understood phrase: a gleaming yellow spire and cross emerging from amongst a cluster of high rise buildings.

Graham Redding had said that if I was interested there was a weekly theological discussion group at the church. Each week a text was circulated and then the group gathered on a Friday night for discussion, preceded by a wine tasting. I went along to the next one. A ring of older people sat under fluorescent lights in the office foyer. People got up and passed the cheese and crackers around while the group tried to identify wines with concealed labels.

'A New Zealand shiraz?'

'Actually seventy per cent cabernet sauvignon, thirty per cent syrah, from Chile'

'Any guesses as to flavour?'

Silence.

'Well it says here ripe berries and chocolate.'

The discussion was on the contested issue (in America at least) of evolution versus 'Intelligent Design', or 'ID'. It was a difficult thing for Christians to discuss, I thought, because they had to process everything at the level of their own deepest belief, their mystical experience, and reconcile it at a cerebral level with the theoretical and political issues. The participants seemed to have a high level of scriptural knowledge. The conversation didn't really flow though, as each person seemed somewhat stuck in their own position. I didn't contribute.

There was a man with a patch on his skull like a square depression, in which shiny, putty-coloured skin lay. The rest of the skin on his skull was also shiny, but pink. His hands were large and swollen, and he talked with one arm around his wife. He rejected the idea that we are more enlightened than our biblical forbears.

'In a museum in Peru I saw a gold plate which had been inserted into someone's skull,' he recounted. 'They'd obviously lived through the operation, as the bone had knitted into the gold.'

We ended with a prayer. 'Dear God, thank you for the gift of intellect, which we can use in exploring issues such as these . . .'

I called up and made an appointment to see Michael Brown, pastor of the Wellington Central Church. He had a sweet, peppy attitude on the phone, saying 'cool', and interrupting himself for some casual banter with a courier.

He came to the door of the church to meet me. He was tall and perhaps chubby under his baggy clothing, with a soft-soled quality and clean floppy hair.

We walked through the low-ceilinged congregational space which I'd already sat in. There were old sofas and painted school chairs arranged in sociable clumps at the back; a future café area, I was informed. The Central Church was evidently doing things on a budget, but its zingy, improvised look seemed like it might be deliberate.

I was introduced to a young man stationed at the reception desk on the way through to Brown's office. In the room next door, a group of young people sat around on sofas with coloured cushions looking like they were having a post-lunch slump.

The office was small, with walls painted electric hues and a glass panel. There was a glossy paperback on Brown's desk with a cityscape on the cover. I read the title upside down. *Why won't they listen?*, it was called. On the wall was an embroidered version of Durer's famous study of praying hands, in shades of caramel.

Brown reiterated for me that they had nothing to do with the original Catholic Apostolic Church begun by William Irving in England, although the Apostolic Church, which had sprung up in Wales in 1904, had also occupied the red brick church for a time. They had been there from 1970 to about 1990, and had dubbed it *Charisma Chapel*.

The Wellington Central Church, its pastor explained, although affiliated to the larger Apostolic Church, operated independently, and was working out how to pay its way. Although the Apostolics had at some stage been centrally financed, in the last twenty years each congregation had been charged with generating its own income. He pointed out that they did not have the luxury of freehold land to build on, as mainline churches often did, like the Catholics their new building out by the Mount Victoria tunnel.

'We didn't have that option so we're using a commercial building, and trying to adapt it as a place of worship.'

This building had belonged to Westpac bank and had been used as a commercial headquarters. When the church took over it was still full of vertical files, bank slips and cheque processing machines.

'At the moment,' Brown explained, 'our trust board owns this building and we've got commercial tenants on the other five levels, but over time, we'll probably take up some space on those levels and use it for small business opportunities. We're trying to create an environment where there isn't so much of a division between the sacred and the secular.

'To help people set up small businesses, or to be in business as a Christian,' he said, 'that's another expression of worship.' He gave the example of the socially conscious breakfast cereal magnate Dick Hubbard's idea of triple-line profit.

'I think we'd be looking for things like not just profitability, but how does this business affect the people who are involved in it in terms of them expressing their potential and giftedness, and also how does this business we're in impact the world in which we live, not only socially but environmentally. You might choose to trade off some profitability because looking after people is more important.

'We're kind of thinking too how can we be missional, within our community,' Brown continued steadfastly, 'and one of the things is a café. Because we think—where do you meet people? If the profit motive is out of it, then it opens up other possibilities. We thought one of the things we could do is provide a free meal once a week. One of the things we got involved in last year was a carol service with the Prostitutes Co-op, which was quite cool. It was done through DrugArm; we just provided the venue.'

Although the pastor believed that 'a church is really

people gathering together, rather than a building', he recognised that traditional church architecture helped people understand theological principles.

'The reason they built those high arches was to draw people's attention heavenwards, because when you stand with that architecture you do kind of look up. A lot of the stained-glass windows were there because people were illiterate, so the story of the gospel was told through the glass, because probably the service would have been in Latin or whatever, so that many of them wouldn't have understood.

'We're on a bit of a journey about how to reach postmodern people,' Brown explained. I didn't really know what he meant by postmodern, but gathered it was the same people *Why won't they listen?* was about. 'I think for a postmodern person, relationship, authenticity, those things would be more important, probably than architecture. But we're coming to see, too, that atmosphere is still really important.'

Perhaps also for the purpose of storytelling, Wellington Central Church had been experimenting with multi-media. A ska band regularly accompanied Sunday services. Brown had recently delivered a sermon which compared and contrasted the *Star Wars* Force with God. They were very similar, he believed, but not quite the same.

'I think often through film,' he said, 'there can be great spiritual truths.'

Church members had recently made a documentary at Victoria University, asking students 'how they felt about the Christian church, spirituality and their own spiritual journey'. I had a look at the short, competent piece, in which Central Church members swooped on students sitting around in the Maclaurin Lecture Theatre foyer. The students were unsurprised at the questions, and although most groped unsuccessfully trying to define the concept of spirituality, each was much clearer about what their own was. Most were agnostic. Only one was 'sometimes' an atheist.

'I'd say at the moment I identify as Pagan,' one well-spoken young woman declared.

As with Graham Redding, the need to keep numbers up was weighing on Michael Brown.

'One of the questions we're asking ourselves is, if we cease to exist as a church would our community even miss that we are here . . . and sometimes I think no they wouldn't.

'Someone came into the church the other day and they said, "Your church looks like a nightclub." I thought, "Is that good or is that bad?" and I thought that's probably good, because one of the things we're wanting to do is create an exchange space, where people come and take another step on their spiritual journey, to faith in God, but also another step in their relationship with one another.'

I asked Brown when he had known he wanted to be a pastor.

'I had a sermon worked out when I was four, based on a cut lunch,' he told me. He couldn't remember the message of the sermon, he admitted, just that the raisins meant one thing, the apple another, and so on.

He explained that he'd grown up in horticulture but

that the chanciness and hardships of cultivating crops was not for him. He remembered when a hailstorm had destroyed a whole season's raspberries on his parents' farm in ten minutes. 'It was like blood running in the aisles,' he said.

I'd called Father Ambrose so many times I knew his number off by heart.

'He surfs the net a lot, so keep trying,' Peter Johnstone's friend had told me when she gave me the priest's phone number.

When he finally did answer the phone, he rushed straight off again, saying he'd left a tap running. Then he came back, and offered plenty of information with cynical asides about the history of the Webb Street building. He spoke with a rambling gusto. I tried to picture him standing somewhere in that murky interior with the soft toys looking out the window.

Father Ambrose had been a Roman Catholic, but as a student at Victoria University he'd converted to Russian Orthodoxy. He'd always wanted to lead a monastic life, he said, and at a certain point he became convinced that the Russian Orthodox Church was 'the one true church'. Never having gone through a reformation, he felt, the Church still had hold of the authentic Christian message.

He gave me an account of the various hands the Webb Street building had fallen into after the Catholic Apostolics had ceased to exist. Through the 1960s the Anglican Maori Pastorate was housed there, with Kingi Ihaka a prominent leader. After that the new, Welsh Apostolic

Church bought the building and it became the *Charisma Chapel*. In 1990, *Charisma Chapel* was sold to the Russian Orthodox Church.

Ambrose imagined that the Apostolics had been unhappy to have to sell to the 'idolatorous' Russians. 'They all drive Lexuses and live in Khandallah,' he dropped in. The sale had almost fallen through, but not quite.

'Money talks,' Ambrose surmised.

Ten years later, when faced with their own dwindling membership and expensive earthquake-proofing requirements, the Orthodox Church considered their buyers. The priest had been reluctant to sell at all, thinking that with fundraising it might be possible to retain the property, but he'd been a lone voice. A Muslim group was turned down. Ambrose muttered something throwaway about terrorists. Instead they passed the church into the hands of the private developer Peter Johnstone, who now lived in the vestry once occupied by Father Ambrose himself.

They'd spent the subsequent years in a former Presbyterian church in Miramar, but were looking to rebuy in the centre of Wellington.

'If you hear of any churches for sale in the inner city . . .' he said.

I asked him what the church had been like when he headed the congregation there. It was very makeshift, he conceded, as it didn't have the structure of a Russian Orthodox church, but it had wonderful acoustics. When I asked him what the music was like, he told me about the differences between Greek and Russian Orthodox churches. The texts are identical, he said, but the Greek music creates a different atmosphere.

'If you want an austere and intellectual atmosphere, go to a Greek Orthodox church; if you want mushy, emotional and sentimental, go for Russian.'

Did he know what the architectural style of the building was? He guessed at it. 'Welsh Gothic—a grandiose, methodist Welsh Chapel,' he thought. 'We're like the hermit crab that climbed into the Apostolic Church's shell.'

When I tried to follow up on some of the things Father Ambrose had told me, I started to understand why nobody knew much about the building.

I called up the Anglican Church, which had apparently absorbed the Catholic Apostolic congregation and taken charge of the building between 1962 and 1970.

'We don't have an archive,' a woman snapped. 'All our papers are with the Alexander Turnbull Library, or you could call our property manager but I doubt he'd know anything.' She was right, and neither did the Turnbull Library.

I called the Anglican Church again. There were columns and columns of numbers under the Anglican Church in the phone. I couldn't see anything that said Maori Pastorate, so I called the office of the Bishop. A man gave me the number for the Right Reverend Bishop Walters.

I called and Mrs Walters passed me to him.

'No, I only came here in 1992,' he said in a posh voice. 'I was in Dunedin before that.'

'Would you know anyone who would have been worshipping in the Maori Pastorate before 1970?' I asked.

'No, sorry,' he said. 'You could call the Wellington Diocese and they might know of the names of some families.'

I called back and got the same man. He gave me an email address.

'Apply to this person in writing.'

I gave up on that and got in touch with Minister Risatone Ete, whose congregation had sometimes held services at the Webb Street church while it was inhabited by the Anglican Maori Pastorate. They had shared a smaller church with a Chinese congregation at the far end of Webb Street. He described his church as 'a warm fellowship of church-going Samoans', and said they had liked using the red brick building. He wasn't able to remember much about the interior, except that it was 'welcoming in terms of surroundings'. He said the best thing about it was that they were able to use the vestry for their after-church socialising.

Father Ambrose had told me the Webb Street church had a twin on Cambridge Terrace. I went to have a look. The building was indeed very much the same as the Webb Street church. It was the same brick structure with white accents, and almost identical cast concrete turrets and steeples. The foundation stone said:

To the glory of God this stone was laid by Hon. George Fowlds 7th Oct. 1916 Rev Archd. E. Hunt Pastor, WM Fielding Architect 1876–1946.

The one document the City Archives had on the Webb Street church was a drawing signed by W.M. Fielding, a sketch of one of the giant wooden trusses with a strengthening rod against it. The Church had apparently been strengthened after the 1942 earthquake. It didn't mean that this architect had designed the church necessarily, although it seemed likely.

I called Jean Prout, the secretary of the Cambridge Terrace Congregational Church, and she allowed me to come and look at the plans Fielding had drawn for their building. I went and sat in her lime green Wadestown kitchen and read through a ring binder of meticulously typed minutes, while she wrote the church newsletter in the next room. It was quiet enough that I could hear her fingers tapping on the keyboard. At one moment the cuckoo clock cuckooed above me. There was nothing very revealing about William Fielding in the file, except that after having designed a building for the Congregational Church he joined it and, possessing a 'rich bass voice', became a valued member of the choir.

Someone suggested that William Fielding might be listed in the Alexander Turnbull Library's biographies index, so I called them up again. Someone else had been after information on this man earlier, and a librarian had written them a letter which was on file. It was a collection of dead ends and meagre findings. Although he was responsible for a number of buildings around Wellington, nobody had deemed him notable enough to write about. The final recorded verdict on his work was 'steady but undramatic'.

What was it about his voice? Phillip Beach, the osteopath Barry Lonergan had told me about, sounded pointedly unfazed. I asked him if I could come over and talk about what it was like living in the red brick church. He assented easily, almost without skipping a beat. In fact, he said, he'd lived in two churches, one in London too.

'Why don't you come to the church, have a cup of tea, and we'll talk about living in churches. How about Monday at five?'

That was easy, I thought. I was imagining I'd need to explain why I wanted to know.

I arrived with a bag of vegan cookies from Aro Café, stood and looked for a moment at the building I'd fixed my attentions on. It was basically a big simple box, with its few Gothic elaborations. The turrets and rose window brought some intricacy to its mass. The bricks were deep in tone, and it looked handsome.

An original Gothic structure from the Middle Ages like Chartres Cathedral is not able to be apprehended all at once, and for all its mass it appears weightless. Almost magically, it defies its own materiality. According to Thames and Hudson's *Victorian Architecture*, Gothic Revival was the default setting for churches at the time of the red brick church's construction. Gothic Revival's more contained, earthy echo of Gothic had come about in a turn of spiritual expression towards romanticism, and a turn of political expression against industrialisation.

This structure was human scale. It didn't dominate. No wonder so many denominations had been able to adapt it to their purposes.

The gates were locked of course, so I pressed the buzzer on the panel of buttons available to the street. Soon Phillip Beach's voice came over.

'It's Anna,' I said, and after a little pause when no voice came back, self-evidently, 'I'm out on the street.'

There was a *yes come in* and the buzz of the gate clicking open. When I reached the door to the apartments between the vestry and the main building, it opened and Beach appeared holding a yellow plastic sack of rubbish, handsome and smiling in the youthful middle age that I equate with people in the healing arts. He wore loose soft olive green clothing and he had an English accent. Evidently he had forgotten about our appointment.

He was apologetic, saying they'd just got back from a tramping weekend in the Orongorongos, insisting it was no trouble for me to come in, and would I mind waiting.

I sat out in the corridor looking at a little planter of parsley on the doorstep of Peter Johnstone's apartment. The open space which once would have been between the vestry and the church had been glassed over and now formed a little lobby. The rougher patina of the original bricks contrasted with the newer materials of the interior passageway: lustrous terracotta tiles, cream paint, halogen lamps and brass apartment numbers on three doors squeezed together at the end of the corridor.

A middle-aged man in a pink shirt and handfuls of hair product came out, setting his alarm and smiling at me as he walked past. The cats I had stroked yowled from inside the apartment for sale.

spheres, you know, that's the type of maths they brought to bear on these churches.'

I couldn't immediately think where to take that, so I went to my list of questions. 'Would you mind me asking what kind of religious upbringing you had?'

He reached into his wallet.

'Mmm . . . I guess I was brought up a normal—' he muttered, and then flipped something out, '—a credit card. That's a golden section rectangle.'

He was deciding which questions were interesting to him, which was fair enough I supposed. He must have sensed that I didn't exactly know what I wanted to know.

He continued, holding up his Visa card. 'That shape is an inherently pleasing shape. It's a specific fraction. It's a fraction where if you divide any one line, say the length of that line,' he pointed to the credit card length, 'there's only one point on that line, about here, where the ratio of the small part to the big part is the same as the big part to the whole thing. And when you start doing this with as ries of lines and connect the corners you come up with spiral, and so, it wouldn't surprise me if this building's sed on that sort of maths.'

I remembered that from *The Da Vinci Code*. The onacci series! I had rushed off and measured the joints someone's index finger to check, and was amazed discover they divided into each other at that precise tion.

Is it possible to articulate what sort of response you to this building when you first saw it?'

Beach reappeared at the door and ushered me into his office. The treatment table was laid out in the middle. Something about the way he sat down and offered me a chair, and asked me what he could do for me, made me think he thought I was here for treatment.

'I'm here to interview you about about living in the church,' I said.

'Right,' he said.

I said again what I had said on the phone, about wanting to find out about the transformation of this space. He went seamlessly into this topic, and I started to wonder if I'd imagined the misapprehension. He asked me if I had come across the original plans of this church. When I said I'd only seen a drawing of a truss and the recent conversion plans, he was not surprised. He thought the Freemasons probably had them.

'The power of the Freemasons was in their ability to build,' he explained, referring to the Middle Ages. 'So all around Europe, for example, original plans for churches were almost impossible to get.'

His office was small, and dominated by books and a massive window which extended up to the level above us. We could only see its bottom half, with its weighty frame and thick stippled glass. The window established a certain ambience: grave but enlightened. A larger-than-life model ear rested on its ledge.

Beach spoke softly and deliberately about the issue of church plans, with frequent pauses, almost as if he were analysing some invisible thing before him and describing it to someone who couldn't see it as he went, or as if he were a doctor, diligently appraising a body and remarking on symptoms.

'It's often like that with churches, and it's something about this hidden knowledge that goes back into Freemasonry.'

'Why do you think the knowledge was hidden?' I asked.

'Because churches were in a sense like . . . weaponry's the wrong word, but, the very best mathematics of the age went into these churches, and they were often a culmination of hundreds of years of maths, science and engineering. They weren't just buildings, they were a bit like an exotic sports car: the best society could produce.'

'Do you think there's such a thing as sacred mathematics?' I asked, thinking that might be putting it mildly.

'Oh absolutely. Oh, that's the whole point of it.' There was a note of either enthusiasm or impatience, I wasn't sure which. He got up and moved towards his bookshelf.

'I can show you some books . . . I might need to go upstairs . . . but, I'm interested in sacred architecture . . .' He perused his office bookshelf. He was excited and distracted by the books.

I tried to say something intelligent.

'I read that in the Middle Ages, the knowledge that enabled those Gothic cathedrals to be built was lost, so that the revivals of Gothic architecture were revivals of decorative features only, for a while, just adorning unremarkable structures. That's until the late Gothic

Revival when technology began to be good enough for the high rise to start developing . . .'

'I don't know.' There was a shortness in his 'When I was in London, there's a very famous ar Keith Critchlow, I've got a book of his somewhe . . . and he was involved with the architectural sc Prince Charles. I went to a lecture of his and he c going down to a church in the South, Le Thoron and over a ten-day period he got out his measuri and measured the church up, because of course get the original plans like usual. I don't think tl I think they're in a vault somewhere. Critch they're in Strasbourg with the head of the F The same with Chartres.

'So he went down there and measurec the lecture was about what he'd discov measurements. He was saying that a thousa in this part of France, there was a meet between the Christian world, the Islami Judaistic world. This abbey was an output o It had architectural elements from the ir three traditions. It was a church designec every four hours, twenty-four hours a dz architecture was around the human voi was a perfect rendition of the human voi

'You see the whole point in those acknowledge God, and acknowledge h and his higher purpose is . . .' He trailec 'As they started to look into maps and started to see golden section rectang

'For me it's a sense of quality, and it's like a labour of love,' he answered. 'It's not just a building, it's that extra that people put into something: it's more than a commercial venture. I like that.'

What was lurking amongst these things: *sense of quality, labour of love, not just a building, more than a commercial venture*? Out of everyone, Phillip Beach seemed closest to thinking the structure carried something in its form.

I tried to take this in a particular direction. 'Do you think it carries some kind of energy from its history of having been worshipped in for a long time?'

'I don't know.' He sounded slightly impatient. 'I don't particularly feel that. I think if that was the case, you'd find it difficult walking anywhere. All places have histories. Particularly densely populated places like Europe,' he laughed. 'People would walk down the street . . . with battles! You know.'

Up until then I had found it curious that none of the people involved in the church knew anything about its history, and none of them had made any kind of effort to ask Father Ambrose next door, who could have told them exactly what he'd told me. When I told Beach what I knew of the provenance of the church, he scribbled it down with interest.

I thought of the house I live in, which is about a hundred years old too, and how I'd never thought to find anything out about it. Every little space in the house is full of what's happening now. Perhaps you have to maintain the illusion that where you live all other histories have vanished, to avert psychic clutter.

The osteopath came back to my question about his religious background, and told me, shorthand, of a trajectory from a mildly Protestant childhood, to time spent in India and enquiries into Buddhism, to where he was now with science pre-eminent among ways to understand the world.

'My sense of spirit is . . . I read *New Scientist* every week. *Scientific American*. I don't believe in fathers and sons and holy ghosts, and virgin births and people dying to save me. For me a sense of spirituality or religion is looking up at the big stars, and a sense of wonder, rather than a brand-name religion.'

'Is your sense of the relationship between all things informed by your profession?'

There was a dismissive 'Mmm . . .' I didn't know whether it was coming from a perfectionist fidelity to the ideas he held dear, that he couldn't tolerate hearing them dealt with clumsily, or from the egoistic need to always be right. I started to feel slightly demoralised.

'I've studied two things,' he told me. 'I've studied osteopathy and I've studied acupuncture. Osteopathy was born a bit over a hundred years ago in the States, by a religious doctor who saw spirit in everything. But that side of the profession I've never really got involved in. Not many have. Then the other profession I've studied is acupuncture and Chinese medicine has got a very very long history, and so I've read Chinese history, I've read about Chinese culture, and I find that . . . quite fascinating.' 'Quite fascinating' was said as an understatement.

Before coming to his place, I'd been hoping he'd

talk about osteopathy, as I'd found the description of its mechanics inspiring. I'd found this explanation on the internet:

> *There is a palpable movement within the body that occurs in conjunction with the motion of the bones of the head. This is a rhythmic alternating expansion and contraction motion in the cranium which is part of the Primary Respiratory Mechanism. This motion exists in every cell of the body and can be felt and worked within any part of the body by a trained physician.*

The synaesthetic melding of sense impressions—cells breathing, gates hearing, bodies filling with light—reveals language as not subtle enough. If music is yellow, there is something in between yellow and music that there isn't a concept for. Whatever moves through us that osteopathy detects seemed like that kind of thing to me. Anyway, I'd missed the boat on that one as Phillip Beach was lukewarm about it. What he really wanted to talk about was Chinese medicine.

He explained what attracted him to things Chinese.

'They had a very different sense of religion,' he said. 'In some way they created themselves. They have less emphasis on gods and more emphasis on their own capacities. All their people seem to be extraordinary humans rather than otherworldly things.

'The research I'm doing at the moment is on acupuncture. They prick you with pins to manipulate your shape,' he said twisting imaginary pins in the air. He took a model of a woman with different coloured lines drawn on her from his desk.

'They don't do many women, mainly men,' he reflected. The lines were carved in, with coloured ink inside them and little holes drilled where the pin pricks should go, with numbers and letters pressed in next to them.

'What's it made from, plastic?' I asked irrelevantly, looking at the yellowish flesh tone peculiar to figurines. He confirmed that it was. The lines ran up and down her body. There was a tan one that went right up the centre, through the middle of her face. A green line intersected it above her top lip. Black lines zigzagged up her legs and travelled up her back, either side of the central tan marking.

'In a sense, this is sacred architecture,' he said. 'The Chinese two thousand years ago came up with this map. From a Western perspective none of those fourteen lines that run up and down the body exist; they're just absolutely invisible. Every single modern scanning technique we've got, from thermal imaging to radioactive tagging to CAT scans and MRI scans—there's nothing there.

'But I think I've cracked that map,' he announced. 'I think I know what the Chinese were mapping, and what these lines mean, and what these lines were a depiction of. It's one of the world's last medical/anthropological mysteries, just waiting to be decoded.'

I thought it might be too complicated or secret to talk about. But he'd already written an article about it, published in the 2004 issue of the *New Zealand Journal of Acupuncture*, and he said he'd lend it to me.

He recounted that he'd worked out how hundreds of muscles work together in various large contractile fields.

Then he'd taken this model and found that it corresponded to the acupunctural meridians.

'It's a good model,' he asserted, 'because when models are good you can take a model from one area and look at another area using the same model. You can take models looking at climate, and you can apply them to the stock exchange, you know, things like that.

'It's the longest article they've published,' he said of his piece in the journal, 'and they don't normally publish non-medical people. The problem I've had, though, is that I'd thought once I'd discovered this, everyone would go "oh, that's obvious", but it's not. When you've got a good idea, you've got to start marketing it. It's another whole . . . skill, another whole dimension.' There was some surprise in this statement.

'It's like, you can build a good church, but then you've got to somehow pull the punters in.'

I thought of the man, every library has a few, who would come in each day to the medical library. He had a theory that New Zealand intelligence had been using snake venom to poison people. Or the Sugarman, who used to come into the museum cafeteria when I worked there, buy one cup of endlessly refillable tea, tip untold sachets of sugar into it, and work among the sugar grains on pencil drawings of pedal-powered machines. It didn't look like anybody was going to reward their efforts.

If Phillip Beach's problem was 'why won't they listen?', there was a strange sense in which he belonged in this building.

'Do you see other things as bodies, like a building or a city?' I asked him.

'Shape. Shape is really important.' This was his response. At that moment it occured to me that perhaps I wasn't interviewing the osteopath at all, but interviewing myself. It was I who saw other things, like buildings or cities, as bodies. He sidestepped my question and invented his own to answer. Perhaps he was doing the same thing in reverse: supplanting me and interviewing himself.

'I can tell you now that those fourteen lines there are based on a very primitive reflex. A reflex that goes back more than five hundred million years, and that's recoil from noxious stimulants. This is a fossilised shark tooth.' He held out a brown glossy shard and pushed into his thigh to demonstrate.

'When you're pricked or burned, you—' he flinched, '—jump away. They discovered there was a pattern to this.' He demonstrated again, pushing himself in the right ribs, his body arcing to the left, pushing in his left ribs, his body arcing to the right.

'So, in totality these recoils hold you in the shape you are?' I asked.

'In a sense, yeah, and in a sense that's what these churches are. These churches were an embodiment of shape, good shape.

'It's border control,' he said. He explained how the black lines on the plastic woman help keep the brown spinal line in its proper place, and how this type of border control is found all through nature.

'To create a border between Russia and China,' he

said, 'you have to have Russians on one side and Chinese on the other.'

He brought it back to people. 'We all know when we're in good shape and in bad shape, and it can be subtle. You can look at yourself in the mirror on a good shape day and a bad shape day and you won't look a lot different, but we get a sense of it. It's often little changes in our shape that we feel aren't right, and the Chinese learnt to manipulate this shape using pinpricks.'

'Do you see those lines on people?'

'It's a bit of both, I can see them and I can feel them.'

There was a pause. Then he started fresh. 'But that's another way of looking at shape. In regard to the church, I think a lot of thought went into shape. They were looking at the archetypes of shape, which is what this esoteric architecture's all about.'

'Do you imagine that it filtered into society?' I asked. 'Do you think that if more people went to the churches that were built with this knowledge of sacred mathematics that somehow it would create a healthier or more spiritually in-tune kind of populace?'

The tone was like he was letting me down gently. 'No, I don't particularly think that.'

'So what's the point?'

'The point was humans trying to emulate something bigger than them. Just a sec, I'll go up and get this book to try to show you what I mean.'

While he was away I thought about an ad I had seen on TV: Roger Federer and Andre Agassi were playing tennis on this leaf-like protrusion, seemingly miles up in the air, jutting out from a glass tower in Dubai. I thought how I wanted to go there one day and see it.

Beach came back with an armful of books, Joseph Campbell on the top. 'I like going back into the roots of things,' he said.

He was pretty sure that a lot of things humans did were motivated by a sense of impending doom. 'You might be a bit young yet,' he estimated. 'But give yourself another twenty or thirty years, and it becomes clear that this game . . . runs out.

'With the advent of technology,' he postulated, 'we started to see there were rules to the way this system was put together, how to make bronze and coppers and iron. In the beginning that was all alchemy, lots of praying and fasting and beating of drums and mixing of different things, and getting fires going . . .'

'You mean like it was more chance and intuition?'

'Well it was *alchemy* . . . it was sort of experiments, but not as we know it. It wasn't the scientific method, but people would work things out, slowly, slowly, slowly.'

'So, now we gain access to the same knowledge through science? That's our way of dealing with the world?'

'Mm . . . no . . .' More frustration. He shrugged away the question. 'I don't want to go into that.'

Somehow the discussion reached a level I couldn't get to. It left me in a strange position, because I found it hard to draw questions out of what he was saying. I gave up trying, and listened to what he had to say.

'I think every scientist knows that there are some extraordinary things; the universe is such a big place, it's just our very parochial way of looking at it that engenders such things as virgin births and the cult of Mary.' He pulled a book from the pile: *Rainforest Shamans: Essays on the Tukano Indians of the Northwest Amazon.*

'Here he is,' he pointed to the cover, a man with a stick drawing circles in the sand, 'probably high as a kite on some kind of hallucinogenic, and he's out there doing his stuff. If we lose the Indians, we lose access to their cultures and their way of seeing the world.'

'Does that make you feel a sense of grief?'

'Oh, it's absolutely terrible. It's everything, you know. Within our lives, there'll be no apes left.

'I'm new to New Zealand, and we were pretty savage when we got to New Zealand. In this whole North Island, you couldn't *walk* anywhere the bush was so thick, and now there's a few pockets left but that's it. All the rest has been reduced to—' (deep inhalation) '—grass and sheep. In battle that would be called a scorched-earth policy. You get the whole ecology and reduce it down to livestock in the hills. And that's what we've done here.'

'How do you live with that, the sense of what's been lost?'

'Well, the more you know about it, if you read, there's a lot out there. In one way it's terrible, in another way it's—I think that piece of writing the *Desiderata*, it's extraordinary.'

I remembered seeing this poem framed with a picture of a waterfall outside the tissue retrieval department at the hospital.

'It's a piece of writing, a chap from last century, an

American man who was . . . I don't know if he'd call himself a mystic, he was just a, good bloke . . .'

He walked out of the room and came back with a small orange book.

'Promise to bring it back but do read it.'

At this moment I registered how much more he had been giving me than I'd asked for. Instead of interviewing himself, I wondered if he'd intuited what he thought I was really asking, and just automatically addressed it.

'He says that the world is evolving the way the world is evolving. It's still a beautiful place. And I suspect that all over the universe animals discover technology, given enough time. And once they discover technology they're like all animals: they take over, and, a bit like the Easter Islanders, they chop down everything until they realise there's nothing else to chop. And towards the end they all get very nasty with each other because they've run out of resources. I imagine that one time in a thousand, their technology is sufficient and, with a lot of luck, their next planet they can do something with. They set off, and their history goes on.'

'Do you think that it's important to have spaces for worship?'

'I guess I do. There are external places or internal places.' By internal I think he meant our bodies and minds. 'If they're external, then you're off on the scenario with the church, which is what all this stuff on geometry's about. See this is this book on the power of limits. Beautiful, extraordinary book.'

He flicked through a book full of line drawings of

animal skeletons and flowers and architecture. It was called *The Power of Limits: Proportional Harmonies in Nature, Art and Architecture.* 'It's that sort of geometry that informed the way churches are built, the way butterflies are built, the way humans are built.

'With that type of work, you start looking at animals—' he showed a picture of a crab, '—and analysing the way they're built, and you end up with all these variants on these types of golden section proportions. And then you start applying it to other animal life and you end up looking at the human form with the same type of approach.

'All these are beautiful statues,' he pointed to photographs of Michelangelo's *David*, 'because they're the ideal human. And then they start applying it to space.

'Here's my business card—' he slipped a card out of his wallet, '—which is a golden section rectangle.'

It was good quality card, mid-grey, subtly waxed on one side. The fine lighter-grey line of a golden section-generated spiral arced over his name and phone number, and enclosed the words OSTEOPATH ACUPUNCTURIST in burgundy. The address was 'Orthodox Mews'.

'That's the maths, I have no doubt, that would inform this church.' He paused, then added, 'They're also very, in a sense, ego-filled things. "Just look at the huge steeple with that unsupported ceiling, and we can build it."'

I wanted to know what Phillip Beach thought about cranial-sacral therapists, who do the same thing as cranial osteopaths but without the medical training. It was medical science versus a form of mysticism. Osteopaths seem to be a bit nonplussed when confronted with the idea of cranio-sacral therapists, like they're charlatans or just delivering some blurry approximation which might succeed by luck.

It was slightly perplexing to me that osteopaths, who have been trained to see this in-between thing, this 'rhythm' which wasn't breathing and wasn't pulse, couldn't imagine how someone could have intuitive access to the same rhythm. There had been a cranial-sacral therapist in the Tintagel community whom people swore by. Beach gave his view.

'There's a lot of debate in the profession about what cranial work is. They proposed these cranial sacral fluids that move through the body, and they suggest that they can feel these fluids, and they can feel bones opening in your skull, and respirating slowly and all this sort of thing. So it's not your pulse and it's not your respiratory rhythm but it's another, quite distinct rhythm. But they don't know really what could power those rhythms. Is it any better than a trained actor? Someone holding your head, saying a few nice things to you . . .'

'Do you think the therapy is some kind of placebo?'

'That's certainly going to be a big part of it. If you have someone concentrating on you for half an hour, touching you very gently.'

This confused me. Where did it fit into science, that thing in which every code is crackable? What was the science of attention, or love?

'The thing about cranial-sacral people,' he elaborated, 'is that they've done an enormous amount of study. They know the twenty-six bones of your skull inside out and backwards; where these bones articulate with each other, the ranges of movement that're possible, the embryology of those bones, how they migrate, how the membranes are that the bones glide on. So they're applying their hands to you. Highly trained hands. So a lot goes on. You're getting someone who's done a lot of training, going into a very quiet space, and feeling someone else. It's two huge biological systems interacting.'

I asked about his patients. 'If you're interacting with this other biological system, do you feel the impact after that?'

'Sometimes. It depends. I think normal people are fairly well defended against other people. If you get too sensitive, you become vulnerable. People who get too open to this stuff find life very difficult.'

'Do you have to work to not get too open to it?'

'I don't know.' He sidestepped himself.

'In the Tibetan tradition they had people that could read minds and all that sort of thing, and go into trances, and have cathartic fits, but these people had to lead very ritually pure lives. They were right on the edge. They had to lead sheltered, careful lives. These shaman, they get schooled, they take drugs, they fast. You often needed a near-death experience to break you open a bit, make you more susceptible, but you lived on the edge of society, you *were* a bit whacko.'

At my request, he took me on a tour. We walked up the stairs from the office in the tube of cream walls and carpeting. Little lights with angled mirrors were at ankle height to provide illumination in the dark.

A piece of amber was resting on a ledge as the stairway turned. Little amulets were all through the house like reminders. A few steps up was an Asian female head. In the bathroom was a primitive figurine with a protuding penis. On the top floor was what looked like a piece of vertebra. In the bedroom, which was quite spartan and almost looked like a storeroom, I noticed none of the usual creature comforts that litter bedrooms. There was a thick mattress on the floor covered with white linen. Heavy flaxen ropes hung above the bed, bearing coathangers full of dark clothing.

'We ran out of space,' he explained.

The top half of an original church window with pointed arch let light into the bedroom level, which had the feeling of a mezzanine. Next door in the bathroom you could peek down between an internal window and the outer church window into Beach's office. The model ear still leaned against the bulky sill.

The stairwell rounded again, ending up on the top floor where the kitchen and living room were. The wooden trusses which had been visible in the rooms below stemmed up through the floor and reached their height. This uppermost level, which reached to the tip of the ceiling, had been created by a sort of running dormer window projecting out of the roof. Beach was happy with the warmth and light on this floor. There was a picture of a man who looked like a fish, or like his face was a puddle, all flattened out, round and liquidy.

'He's the leader of the socialist party in Portugal.' His friend had painted it from TV, he said.

There was a balcony overlooking the controversial motorway bypass, which had cut a swathe through a whole area of historic Wellington. A lone cabbage tree stood against the raw clay being moulded and reshaped by diggers. He felt all right about it, Beach said, although he agreed that he would have preferred other solutions. But, he conceded, they'd done a good job of preserving a lot of the buildings, and progress was at least very rapid. There was going to be a tall green barrier, but he would still see the motorway from his deck, and hear it.

'But after all,' he said, 'we're living in a city.'

A large kayak with a burgundy canvas cover hung from the trusses, looking like an objet d'art. Beach agreed that the wooden beams and window frames gave the place a certain weighty ambience. 'That's why I bought the place,' he said. The trusses in this room, although in upward motion, because of their massiveness and dark tones felt grave, sombre.

He described the other attractions of the apartments. 'I like the fact that it's a small community; it's not a skyrise with 400 people involved. It's six units, we have meetings, we have dinners together and chat. Peter did a very good job designing it; it's very soundproof. So we all live here and have our own independent lives but it's small enough to know everyone by name.'

Graham Redding had laughed when I asked him if he'd like to live in a converted church. He wouldn't have any intrinsic objection to it, he'd said, but he didn't know that it would have been his first choice. He'd thought a lot would depend on what was done with it and whether the contradictions were so 'in your face' that it would actually detract from living there. There are ways to convert old churches and there are ways not to convert old churches, he'd said, although he hadn't been able to articulate what they were. Often though, he'd said, you get a feel for what is a good conversion of space and what is simply a betrayal of the basic aesthetic and architectural qualities that it had.

'I'm glad to bring life back to the church,' Phillip Beach had said, referring to the ability of the developers and apartment owners to maintain the building, when the congregation hadn't.

As I left he told me about a book called *Nisa* and its sequel, *Return to Nisa*. Nisa was a Kalahari bushwoman. The author, after having lived with and written about this woman, returned to wherever she was from, had three children and developed breast cancer. At this point she decided she wanted to return to Nisa, who by this stage was an old woman. The book chronicles all of this, and how she was treated by Kalahari bushmen who went into a trance and put their hands on her. She died of the cancer, nevertheless.

'Sometimes, you know, Western medicine is best,' he said, as I walked out the door.

On my way out, he went back to get my bag of vegan fig chocolate cookies.

'You might as well take these,' he said, without looking inside the bag. 'I won't eat them.' I didn't like to take them back.

'Are you sure?' I asked. 'They're vegan . . . maybe if

you have visitors?' But he insisted. He also said the word 'beautiful', touched my arm kindly, and slightly bowed. I think he meant it was a beautiful gesture.

I walked out into the courtyard, the 'mews', wondering what he did eat, and feeling oddly rejected.

At home later on I read his article. It was pretty difficult for me as a nonmedical person to follow, as he'd predicted. It set out the idea that bodies are governed by fields of primary movement, or contractile fields, to demonstrate the key to the meridial map. Acupuncture's meridian lines map a form of movement—the primitive reflex of recoil from a noxious stimulant. Meridians are therefore 'emergent lines of shape control'.

There was a picture of all these tiny insects sucking on the edge of a great slimy lump. They formed a ring around it. It was deliciously gross. They looked like they were eating it, or trying to pull it. The caption said they were termites and the slimy lump was their queen.

It explained about the limits of the skin the termite helpers were munching on. 'It is a line that is emergent from a myriad of underlying physiological processes that summatively produce the queen's body shape. It is not a line that is discernable in a cadaver. It is not marked by nerve, blood, muscle or fascia. It is only observable in a whole, living, pumped up, queen. It is a line that the termite helpers "feel" for. Meridians have a similar emergent, "feel for" quality. They will not be found on a cadaver.'

In a book I'd been reading about the great rose windows of the Gothic period, the author had talked about how, after the peak years of High Gothic, a certain inexplicable spirit had petered out. After that, the churches built were just geometry and mathematics. The life had gone out of them, or perhaps the holiness. Phillip Beach would not have said *just* geometry.

I called Father Ambrose again and he answered the phone, sounding breathless. I explained my project and said I'd really like to go over the plans with him so he could look at how it was now, and explain how it had been then. I wanted to know how a Russian Orthodox church was organised. I also wanted to ask him about what kind of music they sang, when they had their services, and if everyone sang, or a just a choir.

'Oh yes, you were asking about *space*.' He said it in a way that somehow implied outer space. 'Yeah, if you like,' he said, happily enough but noncommittally. 'But it'll have to wait for a bit. I'm on the waiting list for a bypass and I'm going to get called up any day.

'I'm only doing one or two sermons a month,' he said, after I'd awkwardly showed my concern. 'My cardiologist's already told me I shouldn't be doing any. After a sermon, I'm spent.'

I imagined his sermons would take a lot of energy, although I couldn't imagine the form the energy might take.

'I have to report back to the cardiologist about all these things you see,' he added. 'Next they'll be telling me it's my fault. They're killing off the poor people.' He told me Jenny Shipley had pretty much killed someone once, by saying his lifestyle was to blame for his dialysis and that the government wasn't responsible.

'Wait and see what happens when she needs dialysis,' he said. He talked about the waiting list he'd been on.

'You never know,' he said. 'The Prime Minister might need a bypass tomorrow and you get shunted back on the list.' He laughed and wheezed a little as he talked.

'So it could be any day now?'

'Call me in a week or so,' he said. Wouldn't heart surgery take longer to get over than that? It made me wonder if he was just putting me off.

Before we hung up he asked me if I'd seen Peter Johnstone in the *Dominion Post* newspaper's weekly lifestyle section. 'It's the section called *Indulgence*,' he said, chuckling. There were some pictures of Peter Johnstone's new apartment in the old vestry. Ambrose said he felt envious.

I looked for a postcard I could send him, and settled on a picture of large stalactite and stalamite formations which looked like a cathedral organ.

'Solomon's Temple, Gough Caves, Cheddar,' it said on the back. 'Probably the most magnificent sight in any cave in Europe.'

I had a look at *Indulgence* in the paper.

'An abandoned Russian Orthodox church was the answer to Peter Johnstone's prayer for a city base,' said the strapline. 'Structural consulting engineer Peter Johnstone's impulse buy turned out to have been made in heaven.'

'I knew I could strengthen it easily,' he said.

There was a picture of Peter Johnstone in his bedroom, dwarfed by two of the large stippled glass windows. They were deeply recessed into a white plaster wall. He was photographed from below, wearing black, gazing into mid-distance.

'When he bought the church,' the reporter wrote, 'it was still being used for Sunday services. When he visited, the air would be thick with the smell of incense and wax.'

A few months later, on a Sunday morning, I walked into the Russian Orthodox church on Darlington Road in Miramar. I had found out that Father Ambrose was giving a sermon that day.

The former Presbyterian church was a modernist building, rectilinear in form with pinky brown tinted concrete and not much ornament. It had a richness due to the colour and the softness of age.

Inside, the congregation had found themselves in another large, bare space. The hall was painted a shade of light turquoise, and every feature was utilitarian and simple. Diffuse light came in through large, high casement windows. Rows of circular vents were fitted into the white ceiling. A plywood wainscot lined the entire space, and the floor was light lacquered wood.

The church was full of pictures. They hung salon-style at eye level all around the space. I could see how the Webb Street church would have seemed bereft of atmosphere once these icons had gone.

When I first walked in, there couldn't have been more

than seven people there. A few were clustered around the back table, buying little spherical biscuits in cellophane bags. Father Ambrose was in the middle of them. I recognised the timbre of his voice, his way of breathily exhaling his words, and the constant undertone of satire in them, although he wasn't speaking English, but Russian.

'Hello,' he nodded to me with rushed enthusiasm as I came through the door. He was bustling back up to the sacristy screened off by the altar. As Barry Lonergan had told me, he looked the part. He had a whitish full beard and grey black curling hair scraped back into a scrunched little ponytail at the back of his neck.

He did look unwell I thought—his skin had an opaque whiteness with clouds of pink. He was very animated though, and his eyes, and face in general, were very crinkled with smiling.

I felt out of place and clung mentally to the images lining the walls, perusing them as one might images in an art gallery. I didn't venture further into the space, where the alcoves and altars were.

I could see there was an amazing array of Christ images in many styles. There were shiny faded colour prints buckled in their frames, Byzantine holy families in art deco frames and pictorial wall rugs—a carpetty child's hand clung to a carpetty virgin's robe. Pre-Raphaelite Christs gazed heavenward in soft focus, Gabriels on visitations sat within crimped foil mattes, bright red Saint Georges slayed bright green dragons.

All of the pews had been removed but four at the back. They were rudely constructed, again with light wood, and they would have squeezed in no more than twenty people. This left a huge empty space in more than half the front area, in which the icons were arranged with plenty of space around them, so that you had to physically cross the space to get between them.

It was half an hour after the advertised start of the service. I went and sat as far back as possible. People were still drifting in, talking, collecting and lighting candles. They stumped slender candles into sand-filled cigarette troughs. Some of them nodded at me in a reserved kind of greeting. Three or four had, like me, taken a pew. A woman with a turquoise suit and matching turquoise headscarf trod between the images, lighting candles hanging in front of certain images. I wondered for a moment if the service had already taken place, and I'd been late.

You could see how easily the church's parts could have been disassembled and reassembled. Apart from the many framed images on the wall, they also hung in modular wooden niches which had been arranged to create alcoves. These niches had a folky look, like little gingerbread houses. The wood was decorated with viney arabesques.

Eventually, and all of a sudden, the liturgy began, spoken by another priest. It was a call and response. Everyone crossed themselves at set moments. At a certain point Father Ambrose came through a set of double doors and started to chant a text. His voice was deep and sonorous.

I could hear the sung response, but I couldn't see the lips of the people sitting around me moving. Then I realised that the response voices were coming from behind the right alcove. There can't have been more than four or five people behind there, and they were all women but one. Their voices were thin and faltering compared to his.

I felt sorry for the voices of the people and for the images of Christ. It seemed that each might have felt exposed, that they would have preferred to have sunk into a background, a rich ground, and merged with a field of splendid detail. As it was, the people too seemed in plain view, under the masses of light that streamed in through the large windows. There being so few, each person's movements were sharply obvious. Hard shoes clacked on the light wood floor as a church member went up to cross themself and kiss the edge of three images propped on lecterns dressed with white and apricot satin. Every time the priests went through into the back space, they crossed themselves or kissed the edge of the doorway.

The choir was singing different harmonies. At times the group of voices seemed to splay into incoherence, but then would find a fragile unity. They lurched into unexpected shifts of key which ended up graceful and powerful. Their notes jarred distressingly and chimed alternately with Father Ambrose's more rhythmic monotones. The music went on and on without any sermon. My mind drifted and came back. I forgot that I lived in the Aro Valley with Tony, and that we had a small baby at home who cried and smiled and needed to be fed.

I remembered being taken to church as a child and being seated at the back where the sun caught the dust. What was happening in the front had seemed far away and grey. The hymns and prayer had seemed grey. I remember my own voice seeming loud in my head, and whisperingly singing along. The hymns had seemed hard to grasp. There was no timing to them. Sometimes the notes seemed to last forever, with small words being stretched out, and other times people said a many-syllabled word in one beat, and you couldn't recognise it as the word in the book. There was no way of knowing how long any word would last.

I thought of that moment of fever pitch the men's voices had reached in that Georgian Orthodox Choir CD the student had given me, and how it reminded me of something Tantra had said. Tantra had told me about how I was going to get a sense of something, although she hadn't been able to articulate what it was.

'It's almost like the energy of soot can't be where you are,' she'd said. 'It really has so little to do with circumstance . . . It has more to do with . . .' Then she described a book she'd had when she was a child, with an image of men in a furnace looking at heaven in bliss because they knew they couldn't get burned.

'They knew the furnace couldn't consume them,' she said, 'and I always thought that would be a great way to live.'

I was glad Father Ambrose had become a priest and been able to use that full, round voice. The voices echoed out from the unobserved mouths as if ventriloquising for all the Christs, big and little, hung in the wooden niches in front of them.

I started to really wish I could be in that choir. I started to think about what I'd need to do and how often they practised, and what it would be like at practices with them all speaking Russian. Maybe they wouldn't accept me, I thought, especially since I'm not even a Christian.

If I did try and join, it would be a long project, I realised. I'd have to join the church for a start, and I'd have to learn Russian. I couldn't remember anything from third-form Russian except that while other teachers would wear their black academic robes once annually at prizegiving, Mr Meijers our Russian teacher wore his every single day of the year, and we had to stand up and greet him every time he walked in the room. In class we'd get into pairs and do little set dialogues. '*Kto eta?*' 'Who is this?' the first person would say. '*Eta ya,*' the other person would reply. 'It is me.'

Acknowledgements

To the people who consented to be interviewed or helped with the research for 'A red brick church': Sister de Porres, Bill Mathieson, Peter Johnstone, Barry Lonergan, Graham Redding, Michael Brown, Father Ambrose, Jean and David Prout, Phillip Beach, Chris Cochran, Ron Goulton and Xanthe Martin. To the nine others in Damien Wilkins' 2005 creative writing class; Damien Wilkins, Chris Price, Fergus Barrowman and Ian Wedde. To Elizabeth Sanderson, Isobel Thom, Anna Miles and Luis Jaramillo. To the Young Park Scholarship. And most of all, to Tony McGruddy and to Evie.